HEGEL'S POLITICAL PHILOSOPHY

The Editor

WALTER KAUFMANN is Professor of Philosophy at Princeton University. He graduated Phi Beta Kappa from Williams College in 1941 and received his A.M. and Ph.D. in Philosophy at Harvard University. In 1962, he was named the fourth Witherspoon Lecturer at Princeton, the highest form of recognition that the undergraduate body can officially bestow on a member of the faculty. Dr. Kaufmann has been a Fulbright Professor at Heidelberg and Jerusalem and has lectured widely in the United States and abroad. Among his numerous books are *Nietzsche: Philosopher, Psychologist, Antichrist*; *Tragedy and Philosophy*; and *Hegel: Reinterpretation, Texts, and Commentary*. He has translated many books, including ten of Nietzsche's works, and has contributed many articles to various scholarly journals.

Hegel's

EDITED BY

POLITICAL PHILOSOPHY

Walter Kaufmann

ATHERTON PRESS

New York 1970

Hegel's Political Philosophy
edited by Walter Kaufmann

Copyright © 1970 by Atherton Press, Inc.

Address all inquiries to:
Atherton Press, Inc.
70 Fifth Avenue
New York 10011

Library of Congress Catalog Card Number 79–105606

FIRST EDITION

Manufactured in the United States of America
DESIGNED BY LORETTA LI

Acknowledgment

Richard L. Smith helped me by making copies of the articles in this volume, checking references, reading proofs, and doing most of the work on the Index. It is a pleasure to express my gratitude for his exceptional reliability and heart-warming cheerfulness.

W. K.

Contents

HEGEL'S POLITICAL PHILOSOPHY

Introduction

WALTER KAUFMANN

This volume is intended as an introduction and a contribution to the study of Hegel's political philosophy. The subject has been debated rather heatedly for more than a century, and in many languages. The reasons for this are not hard to find.

First, Hegel was an exceptionally interesting and influential philosopher. Born in 1770, he published his first book in 1807 and did not obtain a professorship until 1816. But during the remaining fifteen years of his life his fame spread far and wide, and when he died in 1831 he not only dominated German philosophy but also left his mark on the study of religion and art, on historical studies, and on political thought. After his death he went into eclipse in Germany, at least as a philosopher. But his influence in the other fields just mentioned remained crucial. Among those whose development simply can-

1

not be understood apart from him are Marx and Kierkegaard. While German philosophers lost interest in him, Hegelianism became dominant in Great Britain and in the United States. Then, early in the twentieth century, when Anglo-American philosophy foresook "Idealism," the Germans rediscovered Hegel. And since World War II interest in Hegel has been growing almost everywhere.

Second, Hegel was an exceptionally difficult philosopher whose interpretation poses monumental problems. Perhaps no other major philosopher is as persistently obscure as is Hegel. There are not merely many dark passages here and there, but almost every page he published requires careful study and reflection before it can be explained with any confidence. Fortunately, he was not particularly prolific; he published four major works: *Phenomenology of the Spirit, Science of Logic, Encyclopaedia of the Philosophical Sciences,* and *Philosophy of Right.* But his students expanded the last two works after his death, adding a lot of material from their lecture notes, and they also published his lectures on the philosophy of history, the philosophy of art, the philosophy of religion, and the history of philosophy—ten volumes in all—always relying on their notes. This material is far easier to read than Hegel's own books, but the texts are not at all reliable. Not only would few professors care to reach posterity by way of their students' lecture notes, but Hegel changed his courses drastically every time he gave them, and his students amalgamated notes taken many years apart and produced a single consecutive narrative. This plan made it necessary for them to supply a lot of their own mortar to fill gaps. Adding further to the confusion, some scholars have come along in the twentieth century and published some of Hegel's early manuscripts that he had refrained from printing. The disparity of all these materials and the obscurity of Hegel's style facilitate widely different interpretations of Hegel.

A miserable cliché says that there are two sides to every question. The implication is that both are equally justified. This is doubly wrong. There are many more than two sides, but not all views have equal merit. Most views tend to be uninformed and incompetent, while a few have sufficient merit to repay close study. Often none of them appears entirely acceptable after careful examination of the evidence and arguments; but those who take the trouble to evaluate several theories stand a far better chance to come up with a good theory of their own than do those who pay no heed to the literature. Many mistakes can be avoided by reading studies that have corrected them some time ago.

The ten essays that follow do not represent ten sides. There are only six authors of whom four appear twice. Two of these four attack Hegel very sharply, along similar lines, while the remaining writers defend Hegel against a large number of charges. Very roughly speaking, then, we do concentrate on two sides after all; but close study should reveal many interesting differences.

Can we say in the end that all these writers are right, or that in the present state of knowledge it is impossible to say who is right? Neither verdict is tenable. It is not as if all sides agreed about what Hegel actually said and the dispute was mainly about whether he was right. It is actually surprising how little argument we find in these pages about what is right or wrong, good or evil. Most of the disagreements are about whether Hegel did or did not say this or that. And that kind of question can usually be decided by careful scholarship. But in that respect some of the pages that follow are rather disappointing. Indeed, one is sometimes led to wonder whether old errors never die.

THE MARCH OF GOD AND OTHER BONERS

One alleged quotation from Hegel that keeps cropping up in these pages is said to be found in section 258 of *The Philosophy of Right*. The sentence in question, however, is found only in the posthumous edition where it is clearly marked as an editorial addition, based on lecture notes. The editor, Eduard

Gans, explained in his preface that in these additions "the stylistic order, the connection of the sentences, and sometimes the choice of words as well are mine."

In German the sentence reads: *"Es ist der Gang Gottes in der Welt, dass der Staat ist."* In his *Hegel Selections* (1929), J. Loewenberg mistranslated these words without even indicating that they came from an "Addition," as follows: "The State is the march of God through the world." But even if the German text had *das* (with one s), this neuter pronoun could not possibly refer to *Gang* which in German is masculine. *Dass* is no pronoun at all but a conjunction, and the correct translation is: "It is the way of God with [literally: in] the world that there should be [literally: is] the state." The point is that the existence of states is no mindless accident but, metaphorically speaking, God's plan or providence, and it is the philosopher's task when discussing this institution to discover its reason, its *raison d'être.*

"The march of God in the world, that is what the state is," writes Knox in his generally admirable translation, and Hook echoes this version. But this interpretation is also totally untenable; it founders on the facts already mentioned. Incidentally, *gehen* means *go*, and *Gang* means *way*; and the importation of *march* speaks for itself.

This misquotation is first encountered in the following pages in Carritt's initial reply to Knox (see page 36). It is followed by several more quotations in the same paragraph, and most readers probably would not notice, and Carritt himself may have overlooked, the fact that none of these proof texts was published by Hegel himself.

The first comes from *System der Sittlichkeit,* written by Hegel around 1802, five years before he published his first book and about twenty years before the appearance of *The Philosophy of Right.* This "System" was first published as a whole by Georg Lasson in 1913, in Hegel: *Schriften zur Politik und Rechtsphilosophie* (2d rev. ed., 1923). The sentence about "The absolute government" quoted by Carritt is found on pp. 483f.—and in context does not mean anything like what Carritt takes it to mean. In his introduction, Lasson had explained: "This is followed, under the title 'the absolute government,' by the description of a form of government that could most nearly be designated as theocratic—the rule of the priests and the old. . . . Real governments are discussed only in the next chapter about 'general government' " (xxxix f.).

Or take the last quotation in that paragraph, taken from Lasson's edition of Hegel's lectures on the philosophy of history. Again a totally misleading impression is given to the reader, as will be evident immediately when we cite the first sentence that has been omitted in the middle. (The omission is duly marked by three dots.) "Those who in ethical determination and thus nobly resisted that which the progress of the idea of the spirit made necessary are superior in moral worth to those whose crimes would have been transmuted in a higher order to become means that would implement the will of this order." Hardly a stylistic gem, but sufficient to show that Carritt's proof texts do not say what he takes them to say. For further discussion of this idea, see the last essay, below.

It would not be feasible to offer at this point a catalogue of errors. Sooner or later many claims in these pages are challenged, some only in the final essay. But anyone who perseveres to the end and then, after the last chapter, goes back to some of the preceding attacks might find that an interesting experience.

NATIONALISM

The article on "Hegel and Nationalism" is very informed and illuminating but contains one striking error that is interesting enough to be briefly considered here. Hegel was even much less of a nationalist than Avineri suggests in the second paragraph of section V, when he says: "Now, it is true that the formal division of the *Philosophy of History* into oriental,

Greek, Roman, and Germanic periods points to the interpretation of epochs characterized each by a different dominant
nation."

This concession is perplexing. Hegel divides history into
three, not four, eras, and not one of these is characterized by a
dominant nation. "Oriental" means for Hegel the whole realm
from China and Japan to Mesopotamia and Egypt; the Greeks
and Romans he lumps together, and even if he did not it would
be far from clear that either the ancient Greeks or the old
Romans could be considered a nation; and the Germanic peoples who inhabit Protestant northern Europe are obviously not
a nation.

HOOK'S FINAL REJOINDER

Hook's final attack on Hegel's "apologists" poses a difficult
problem for the editor. To omit this statement would seem
unfair and unjustifiable in a volume devoted to controversy;
but letting it stand as the last word does not seem right either
and would be unfair to Hegel and his "apologists."

To some extent the problem is solved by including at the
end of this volume two earlier articles in which some of Hook's
points are discussed at length. But he raises many other points
that are not discussed elsewhere in these pages. To hunt down
every issue and offer, as it were, a school solution in the end
would be out of keeping with the spirit of this series. But a word
about the nature of controversies seems entirely appropriate.

Ideally, the opponents in an intellectual discussion should be
concerned above all to illuminate the issues and to bring to
light the truth. In fact, there is always the temptation to
develop a vested interest on one side of a debate and to try
to score off one's opponents, even to destroy them—not only their
arguments but their credibility and reputation.

Sidney Hook's rejoinder goes rather far in yielding to this
temptation. In the very first sentence he compares his opponents to "circle-squarers." Any reader who might have won-
dered whether Avineri's expertise on Hegel did not perhaps

exceed Hook's is thus advised to think of Hegel's "apologists" as a bunch of nuts, while Professor Hook reminds us that he had made "no startling claim." Nobody had said that his claims were startling. The question raised by Avineri was whether Hook had repeated "some of the misconceptions which have bedeviled this discussion in the past two generations." Hook begins by setting aside the question whether these old charges against Hegel might deserve to be given up. Instead we are given the impression that Hook is a very sober and unemotional man who is opposed by some irrational extremists.

But by the end of section 2, Hegel is charged with "the most specious reasoning that ever disgraced a philosopher" and his writing is "nauseating." In section 4 "Hegel's ignoble behavior" is mentioned—but strong language is substituted for evidence. In the following section Hook calls Avineri's procedure "intellectually scandalous." By section 5, J. F. Fries has been turned into a liberal (for some quotations from his political writings of that period see section 5 of the last essay in this volume) and we are told that "Hegel sicked the police on to Fries." Hook has said this more than once without substantiating his charge. There is more of the same, and in section 7 "Hegel is the very model of a small-minded, timid Continental conservative." Small-minded indeed!

That Hegel was timid is proved eventually by a quotation from a letter to a friend in which Hegel said that he was *ängstlich* and loved *Ruhe*—that he was anxious and loved peace and quiet. Heaven help him had he said in a letter that he loved the clang of battle! Surely he was not timid as a thinker.

In the end Hook admits that Hegel's insights are independent of his personality—but concludes by saying once more that his personality was not "very admirable." Why this concern to blacken Hegel's admittedly irrelevant character? Professor Hook sounds like a district attorney, not like a philosopher. At that, he sheds little light on Hegel's personality. Having tried in my *Hegel* to offer among other things a portrait of the man, I shall not say another word here about his character or life.

LIBERAL OR CONSERVATIVE?

There is another issue with which Hook is greatly concerned, and some of the other writers in this volume also touch on it. This is the question whether Hegel was a liberal or a conservative. Since none of the combatants offers any definitions of these notoriously ambiguous terms, the question strikes me as rather pointless. It seems that the participants in this debate consider it good to be liberal and bad to be conservative, and that they disregard the awkward fact that these labels have different meanings in different countries and at different times.

"Liberal" rabbis in Germany between the first and second World Wars were distinguished by the very stance that marks "conservative" rabbis in the United States: observing the dietary laws and the Sabbath, conducting their services entirely in Hebrew, and having men and women sit separately during services. Both occupied the center between orthodox Judaism and Reform.

In England the two labels bring to mind two political parties, and a Conservative of the sixties may well favor policies considerably to the left of those advocated by the Liberals a few decades earlier. In the United States the two terms have no clear application at all, although a great many professors made a point of being "liberal" before the radicals of the late sixties did their best to make "liberal" a dirty word.

From the following pages we gather that Paine and Jefferson were liberals, but we are left in the dark about Washington, Madison, and Hamilton whom neither label seems to fit very well. And how would one establish that Paine was a liberal rather than, say, a radical? (Paine is mentioned once by Pelczynski and not at all by Avineri, but Hook discusses him at length to suggest that he was a liberal while Hegel was not.) And was Jefferson a liberal regarding revolution? Was he a liberal about slavery? Was not Hegel much more liberal than Jefferson about slavery?

Such "ism" words are an impediment to philosophic thought and historical understanding. *Philosophy begins beyond "isms."*

BACK TO HEGEL

Whoever wants to know what Hegel's political philosophy really was, must in the end go back to Hegel himself and read above all *The Philosophy of Right*. But Hegel is far from easy, and many readers get lost and do not know for what to look. This volume of controversy may add a dimension to the study of Hegel. It should alert students to issues and problems and bones of contention that they might otherwise overlook. And it may help scholars, too, by showing them what can be said, and actually has been said, against interpretations that had seemed reasonable to them.

Sometimes debates like these are depressing. But they also explode the prejudice that scholarship is bound to be lifeless and dull. Or that scholars are not human—all too human.

I The First Debate

1 *Hegel and Prussianism*

T. M. KNOX

      Despite the efforts of Bosanquet,[1] Muirhead,[2] Basch,[3] and many others, it is still frequently stated or implied, in both popular and scholarly literature, that Hegel (a) constructed his philosophy of the State with an eye to pleasing the reactionary and conservative rulers of Prussia in his day,[4] and (b) condoned, supported, and, through his teaching, became partly responsible for some of the most criticized features in "Prussianism" and even of present-day National-Socialism.[5] In this article I propose to give reasons for denying (i) that Hegel the man is justly accused of servility to the Prussian Government, and (ii) that there is any warrant in the text of his *Philosophie des Rechts* for the charge that Hegel

The first four papers in this volume originally appeared in *Philosophy* (England), January, April, and July, 1940.

the philosopher was an exponent of "Prussianism" and "frightfulness."

I

After occupying a philosophical chair at Heidelberg for two years, Hegel was appointed Professor of Philosophy at Berlin in 1818, and delivered his Inaugural Lecture on October 22nd. During the winter he lectured on "Natural Law and Political Science" (*Naturrecht und Staatswissenschaft*) as well as on his *Encyclopaedia,* and at this time or a little later he must have started to write his *Natural Law and Political Science in Outline, or Fundamental Principles of the Philosophy of Law*[6] (*Naturrecht und Staatswissenschaft im Grundrisse— Grundlinien der Philosophie des Rechts*) as a textbook for future courses of lectures on this subject, which really comprised jurisprudence, ethics, and political philosophy. The book was not published until 1821. The evidence that he started to write it shortly after his arrival in Berlin is contained in a letter from him to Friedrich Creuzer, formerly his colleague in Heidelberg. Creuzer had sent to him a copy of the new edition of his work on ancient mythology, and Hegel replies (October 30, 1819) that his acknowledgment has been delayed because he had hoped to send as a return—though too poor a return— "some sheets of my §§ on the Philosophy of Law." He had been ready to go to press with his book when the Carlsbad decrees were issued. "Now that we know where we stand with our exemption from censorship, I propose to print at once."[7] Since the *Philosophie des Rechts* is divided into sections, it is plain that it is to this book that Hegel refers. To enable us to understand the rest of his statements, a short excursion into history is required.

The Congress of Vienna which settled the map of Europe in 1814 was a triumph for conservatism, for diplomats to whom the revolutionary ideas emanating from France were anathema. It was a defeat for Stein, who for years had labored to make the Germans a united people, and who by his reforms had tried to give them civil and political liberty. He retired into private life, but it was his ideas which led in 1815 to the formation of a German Students' Association with "Honour, Liberty and Fatherland" as its motto. Two years later some hundreds of students from all over Germany held a festival on the Wartburg as a demonstration in favor of freedom and German unity. Fries, Hegel's predecessor in his Heidelberg chair, was one of the speakers on this occasion, and his enthusiastic address is the subject of some criticism in the preface to Hegel's *Philosophie des Rechts.*

In 1819 Kotzebue, the writer, was murdered by a student named Sand on suspicion of being a Russian spy whose activities were inimical to the cause of German liberty. This event caused such a sensation that the Governments of the German States felt that they now had an opportunity to take action against revolutionary ideas prevalent in the universities. After a conference at Carlsbad they issued what are known as the "Carlsbad decrees" on September 20, 1819. These provided for a strict censorship of periodicals and pamphlets as well as for the suppression of the Students' Association. At the same time Fries was dismissed from his chair at Jena. On October 18th university teachers in Prussia were officially made aware of the decrees, and they were also informed that *all* their publications would be censored; the exemption from censorship which the Prussian universities, together with the Prussian Academy, had enjoyed would now be suspended.

It is clear from what Hegel says to Creuzer that his book on the *Philosophie des Rechts* was completed by September 20, 1819, the date of the Carlsbad decrees. Between that date and October 30th, the date of Hegel's letter, he had been officially informed of the position about the exemption from censorship hitherto enjoyed by university professors, i.e., he had been informed that the exemption was suspended; but now that the atmosphere of uncertainty had passed he proposed to go ahead with his book and submit it to censorship in the ordinary course. The manuscript was sent to the publisher, and some of it may even have been printed at this time, because there is a receipt, signed by Hegel and dated December 15, 1819, acknowledging a payment on account of royalties on his forthcoming book on *Naturrecht*.[8] On second thoughts, however, he must have decided to withhold the book until the excitement arising from Kotzebue's murder had died down, because the date appended to the preface is June 25, 1820, while the date on the title page is 1821.[9]

What emerges from these facts is that (i) despite the title-page date, Hegel's book was begun almost as soon as he arrived in Berlin. This might at first sight lend plausibility to the conjecture that, on entering the service of Prussia, he decided to write a book on political philosophy supporting the Prussian *status quo*. But his interest in the subject was not new in 1818; it had been a dominant one ever since his student days. Nor were the conclusions embodied in his book new in substance. His opinions developed, as one might expect, with advancing years; but there is no radical change. From first to last he is fascinated by what he regarded as the unity of Greek life, and his problem remains the same: How is it possible to combine the individual Greek's complete devotion to his city with the modern emphasis on the paramount importance of individual freedom? There is hardly anything in the *Philosophie des Rechts* to surprise a reader of Hegel's earlier writings on political philosophy; in particular, the theory of the State contained in the book published in 1821 is simply a working out in detail of the material already contained in the relevant portion of the *Encyclopaedia* of 1817. Hence there is no ground for supposing that, when Hegel went to Prussia, he began by reconstructing his philosophy of the State to suit the mind and practice of his new masters.

(ii) The reason why publication was delayed for eighteen months after the book was ready can hardly have been anything except fear of the censor. But if it had been written to gratify the Prussian Government, how could he have had such fears? Their very existence implied that his book contained matter which might be unpalatable to the authorities on the score of its liberalism.

How did Hegel overcome any difficulty that might have been expected from the censor?[10] Two courses were open to him. He might have revised his book and accepted Prussian conservatism; or he might have written a preface explaining that, while his ideas were more liberal than those of his Government, he shared its opposition to revolutionary ideas and the dangerous excesses to which they might lead their advocates. It was the latter course which he actually chose. The preface, however, has been called "servile" because it (i) denounces Fries, (ii) condemns the Wartburg Festival, and (iii) by identifying the real with the rational, justifies the *status quo*.

(i) Now it may be admitted that, in writing as he did, Hegel had his eye on the censor; and it was a cruel thing to attack Fries—a former colleague as *Privat-Docent* in Jena—when he was in disgrace and suffering personal hardship. But is Hegel using servility, or is he using legitimate explanation of his own independent position in order to satisfy the censor? "The latter" is the only answer which fits the facts.

His poor opinion of Fries was of long standing. In 1811, on the publication of Fries's *Logic,* he jotted down his impressions of the book: "Superficiality, vague chit-chat—wholly platitudinous—trivial argumentation, like that used to children—empty narrative, devoid of philosophic precision, etc."[11] These unpublished remarks are more sweeping than those in the preface to the *Philosophie des Rechts,* but their content is the same. The criticisms of Fries in this preface were thus not made to order; nor were they the first criticism of Fries which Hegel *published.* There is a caustic footnote about him in the introduction to the *Science of Logic,*[12] published in 1812.

(ii) If Hegel's attack on Fries is nothing new, is the condemnation of the Wartburg Festival a departure from his convictions in order to please a censor? At first sight it may seem that it is. At this festival the writings of von Haller were burned, and in the body of the *Philosophie des Rechts* (§ 258) there is a trenchant criticism of von Haller's book—"this welter of crudity." The Festival was a demonstration in favor of liberty—the *leit-motiv* of Hegel's book—and German unity, of which he was the prophet in his essay on the German Constitution, written in 1802, though not published until 1893. But it is not the objects of the Festival to which he raises objections in his preface; it is the methods adopted to obtain them. Feeling and enthusiasm, he holds, are dangerous guides: in this instance they led to the murder of Kotzebue, and murder, however conscientiously committed, is still murder. This is the theme of much of the second part of the *Philosophie des Rechts,* and the condemnation of the Wartburg Festival follows from the argument there; the assumption of adaptability to a conservative régime is not required to account for it. The Festival is specifically condemned in the preface in order to obviate the misunderstanding that the only alternative to von Haller, condemned in the body of the book, is Fries.

(iii) The statement that "the real (*wirklich*) is the rational" was misunderstood by some of Hegel's contemporaries to imply that what exists (e.g., the Prussian State) is rational, and he inserted some explanatory sentences into the second edition of the *Encyclopaedia* in 1827 in order to remove the misapprehension. It should have been clear, however, to readers of the *Philosophie des Rechts* that, whatever Hegel meant by his identification of the real and the rational, he did not mean to justify the *status quo,* because the rational State described in the third part of his book was not a description of any State actually existing at that time. (It is sometimes said to have been a description of Prussia, but the differences are so striking, as we shall see in Part II of this article, that no contemporary of Hegel's could reasonably have made such an assertion.) Hegel doubtless gave a meaning of his own to the word *wirklich,* and he had explained this meaning as early as 1812 in the *Science of Logic,* but it could have been gathered by an attentive reader from the *Philosophie des Rechts* itself (e.g., Preface and § 1) without knowledge of Hegel's other books.

Against this view that the preface is simply explanatory of Hegel's general position in the body of his book, and not "servile," there is sometimes adduced a sentence which occurs in it as follows: *Bei uns die Philosophie . . . eine öffentliche, das Publikum berührende Existenz, vornehmlich oder allein im Staatsdienste, hat* ("with us—i.e., in Prussia as distinct from Greece—philosophy has an existence in the open, an existence in touch with the public, an existence principally or only in the service of the State"). What does Hegel really mean here? Mr. Carritt, for instance, interprets the words as an assertion that "the proper exercise of philosophy is in the service of the State,"[13] or that "philosophy is to be the servant of the State."[14] Now since Hegel, in the *Encyclopaedia,* ascribes philosophy to the section on Absolute Mind, which transcends Mind Objective, the section in which the State appears, it would be odd if he were to maintain in the *Philosophie des Rechts* that the higher is the servant of the lower. What Mr. Carritt's interpretation seems to overlook is the sense in which Hegel normally uses *Existenz*. In speaking of the *Existenz* of philosophy he is speaking of philosophy's existence as an institution, as an organization in the objective world. The difference between Prussia and ancient Greece, so far as philosophy is concerned, is that in the former philosophy is an organized study in the universities, whose professors are *ex officio* civil servants, i.e., "in the service of the State." Hegel is simply stating an obvious fact about philosophy as an organized study in Prussia; he makes no assertion about the *"proper exercise"* of philosophy or about what philosophy *"is to be."* I can find nothing in the German to justify Mr. Carritt's use of the words italicized, and nothing in Hegel's meaning to justify a charge of servility against him on the strength of his use of this phrase.[15] There is no "servility" in holding that, if a civil servant cannot reconcile his philosophy and his political allegiance, he should demit his office, if his office consists in teaching philosophy.

The question whether Hegel was a man of a cringing disposition is relevant to a consideration of the charge that he truckled to the Prussian Government. To answer such a question a whole biography would be required, but reference may be made here to some of Hegel's actions during his Berlin period (1818–1831) when he was at the height of his powers and his fame, and when he was being accused of servility by Fries and others who were jealous of his success. In youth he had been an enthusiast for the French Revolution as the assertion in practice of man's natural right to freedom. In 1826, on the anniversary of the taking of the Bastille, he drank a toast with his students in honor of the event; "he explained its significance and said that a year never passed without his celebrating the anniversary in this way."[16] In youth he had advocated the unification of Germany; in Berlin he remained faithful to this ideal and had not forgotten that he was a South German himself. In 1826, for instance, when he founded his *Jahrbuch für wissenschaftliche Kritik,* he endeavored to secure the cooperation of Bavarian scholars and hoped that the periodical might help the cause of German unity.[17] When he was leaving Heidelberg for Berlin he said in his letter of resignation that he hoped, in going to Prussia, to have administrative as well as teaching responsibilities.[18] Perhaps he hoped to have charge of the Academy or to have some share in the Ministry of Education, but any such hope was vain. If he was so sound a conservative as some have held, why was he never given such an administrative post?

When his colleague de Wette was dismissed from his chair for writing a letter of sympathy to the mother of Kotzebue's murderer, Hegel was one of the subscribers to a fund to help him in pecuniary difficulty.[19] He brought with him from Heidelberg an assistant, Carové, whose membership of the Students' Association made him suspect to the Faculty in the University as well as to the Government, and Hegel was forced to dismiss him. In his place he appointed von Henning, but it took him ten weeks to get the appointment confirmed, because von Henning also was suspected of demagogic sympathies. In 1820 he went bail for a student arrested on suspicion of disaffection.[20] Another Berlin student was for the same reason inhibited from attendance at the University in 1819. He appealed to Hegel for aid and, despite Hegel's continued efforts, his reinstatement could not be secured. When he was eventually reinstated in 1823, it was not Hegel's but another's pleadings which secured this result. Von Wittgenstein, von Kamptz, and other "demagogue-hunters," who might with some fairness be called "servile," attacked Hegel and attributed the "disordered" minds of students in part to the unhealthy "mysticism" and "pantheism" of his philosophy.

It is difficult to fit facts like these—and Dr. Hoffmeister adduces others—into a picture of Hegel as a reactionary conservative, the trusted ally of the Prussian régime. Like other men, he had his faults, but servility was not one of them.

II

So far we have been concerned with Hegel the man and his relations with the Prussian Government. We now turn to the *Philosophie des Rechts* in order to discover whether it actually contains adulation of Prussia or approval of those aspects of Prussianism and National-Socialism which are commonly criticized in this country. If it did contain these things, it would be hard to explain why Hegel's influence in Germany waned so rapidly after his death, or why his works went out of print during the heyday of Prussianism. English readers sometimes forget that when Hegel was being translated into English in the 'nineties of last century his philosophy was dead in Germany.

The rational State which he describes in the last part of the *Philosophie des Rechts* is not, he explains, any existing State; political philosophy is not the same as the empirical study of political institutions. Yet he is often said to have identified the rational State with the Prussia of his own day. This is impossible; the differences between what he regarded as "rational" political institutions and those under which he actually lived are too many and too striking. Three of them may be briefly mentioned here: [21] (i) He holds that "subjective freedom" requires trial by jury; questions of fact should be settled by the defendant's peers (§§ 219 ff.). In Prussia there were no trials by jury when his book was published. (ii) He advocates parliamentary government, and is at some pains to describe in detail the constitution of the two Houses and the manner of appointment of their members. Further, he advocates the publicity of their proceedings—all this in the interests once more of "subjective freedom." He is a supporter of monarchy, but only of monarchy of a kind so limited (*constitutionelle Monarchie*) as to be compatible with liberty; i.e., although the monarch is at the head of the State, his functions are to be restricted; he is one organ of the body politic, the executive and the legislative being the other two (§§ 275–315). Prussia in Hegel's day was an absolute monarchy, and the Estates did not meet as a Parliament. Stein had proposed to give Prussia a "Constitution," but it did not receive one in Hegel's lifetime. (iii) He argues for the freedom of the Press and allows the expression of public opinion. It is true that he thinks there are limits to this freedom, but the important point is that he does hold that personal freedom is robbed of its rights if the individual is not at liberty to hold opinions of his own and to utter them (§§ 316–319). We have seen already in this article that such freedom was not enjoyed in the Prussia of his day.[22]

Hegel thought that Plato had described in the *Republic* not a Utopia or a castle in the air, but the rational essence (the τι ην ειναι) of Greek political life, and in more than one place he develops his own views in contrast with Plato's in a way which suggests that he was trying to do for the modern world what he took Plato to have done for Greece. His rational State, then, is a description of the essence of modern political life, exemplified to some extent in existing States, however bad, just as the essence of manhood is exemplified to some extent even in the cripple. Now he holds that in anything finite there may be a discrepancy between what it is implicitly and what it is overtly; e.g., a man is a man, as distinct from an animal, in virtue of his rationality, and implicitly or in essence or in principle any particular man is rational; actually, however, he may act in defiance of this rationality, though he does not thereby cease to be man, i.e., he remains rational in essence. If he learned, however, that rationality *was* his essence, and believed this, he would bring his conduct more into line with his genuine manhood, i.e., his rationality. Similarly, a bad State is still a *State* only because the conception or the essence of political life works within it; and if it comes to recognize that its actual institutions or actions clash with the conception or essence which makes it a State, it will proceed to reform itself and bring itself more into accordance with that conception or essence. It is this essence which Hegel describes in the *Philosophie des Rechts,* and his book amounts therefore to an invitation to statesmen to reform their States in accordance with his principles, principles which he professes not to have invented but to have discerned already at work (*wirkend,* i.e., *wirklich*) in varying degrees within existing States, and in virtue of that fact entitling them to be called States. It is, then, a precise reversal of the truth to regard Hegel's book as a justification of the *status quo.*

But surely, it will be said, even if this interpretation be sound on the whole, still there are detailed passages in Hegel's book where he (i) asserts or implies that might is right, (ii) defends the suppression of freedom of conscience, and (iii) holds that the individual is a mere means to the State's ends. (i) Mr. Carritt, for instance, says that by adopting Schiller's epigram, *Die Weltgeschichte ist das Weltgericht*, Hegel "frankly identifies might with right."[23] It is true that the epigram might be adopted by a thinker who intended to make this identification, but did Hegel intend to make it? In the *Philosophie des Rechts* (footnote to § 258) he distinguishes between von Haller's advocacy of the rule of the mighty, or the rule of force, and his own doctrine that it is the right which is in the long run mighty. What triumphs in history, he thinks, is the right or God's purpose, the rightness of which is intrinsic to itself, not dependent—as the might is right doctrine implies—on its might. (See, e.g., the closing paragraph of his *Philosophy of History,* where he contends that the true theodicy is the demonstration, provided by the philosophy of history, that the history of the world is the process of the realization of *Mind,*[a] not force or might.) Hegel's belief that it is possible to discern in history a progressive development—a development of mind— is doubtless open to numerous difficulties, but it is to turn his doctrine upside down to hold that he thinks that the triumph of one "world-historical" nation over another is a triumph of mere brute force (or *Naturgewalt*) when he thinks in fact that it is the triumph of reason. Had he held that might was right because it was mighty, he would surely have advocated despotic government, or absolute monarchy. As it is, when he treats of sovereignty (§ 278) he clearly distinguishes, like Aristotle, between the sovereignty of a despot who rules by whim, and so by force, not by law—the type of sovereignty which he rejects—and the sovereignty of limited monarchy which implies law and constitution, and so rests on rationality, not whim or force—the type of sovereignty which he advocates. He speaks there of the common misunderstanding which confuses might with right and tries to remove it, but despite his plain words, he seems so far to have failed to convince some readers that he himself distinguished these two conceptions and gave priority to the second.

(ii) While he repudiates the doctrine that might is right, he does not repudiate freedom of conscience. He specifically allows conscientious objection to service in warfare (second footnote to § 270) and speaks of man's conscience as a "sanctuary which it would be sacrilege to violate" (§ 137). It is true that this is not his whole teaching about conscience; it is not enough, he thinks, that a man should be conscientious; mere conviction does not ensure infallibility.[b] To be justified a man must be conscientiously convinced of what is inherently right (§ 141). This, however, is a long way short of advocating the suppression of conscience altogether.

---

[a] Hegel's *Geist* should be translated "spirit," not "mind." Often, as here, "mind" misses the point. Cf. Zechariah 4.6: "Not by might, nor by power, but by my Spirit." w.k.

[b] See section 8 of Kaufmann's essay, below. w.k.

(iii) But did Hegel not maintain that the individual was a mere means to the ends of the State? Mr. Carritt confidently gives an affirmative answer,[24] though it seems to me that Hegel's own answer is negative. Not once only but repeatedly in the *Philosophie des Rechts* (Preface and §§ 46, 185, 206, 299) Hegel criticizes Plato, and each time the point of his criticism is that in his Republic Plato did not allow enough freedom of choice to the individual. He objects to Plato that he makes the State everything, the individual nothing (*Zusatz* to § 184), that he stifles individuality by denying private property and family life to the guardians and by refusing to allow members of the lower classes to choose their own walk in life. Self-subsistent individuality, Hegel continues, was unknown to the Greeks and was introduced into the world by Christianity, and it is to make room for this principle in his State that he advocates, e.g., a parliamentary constitution and facilities for the expression of public opinion. Whether his criticism of Plato be justified or not is not here in question, but the fact that it is directed against Plato's alleged subordination of the individual to the State is surely sufficient reason for refusing to ascribe to Hegel precisely what he asserts is Plato's chief error.[25]

The view here put forward that Hegel rejects the doctrine that might is right, allows freedom of conscience and does not make the individual a mere means to the ends of the State is supported by his explicit statements in the passages already cited. These statements, moreover, are not mere incidental remarks or casual phrases inconsistent with his main doctrine: on the contrary, they are integral to that doctrine itself. He tries to find a place in the State *both* for individual liberty *and* for strong government, and he holds that it is a sign of the strength and depth of the modern State that its subsistence is compatible with allowing its particular members to develop to "self-subsistent individuality" (§ 260). His political doctrine of the State and the individual accords with his logical doctrine of the universal and the particular and his metaphysical doctrine of the infinite and the finite. The all-powerful State in which the individual counts for nothing, or which "absorbs into itself the strength of its individual members" (*Zusatz* to § 184), would, in his view, be just an analogue of Schelling's Absolute— "the night in which all cows are black." In the *Philosophie des Rechts* he attempts to steer a course between the Scylla of individual license on the one hand and the Charybdis of despotism on the other, and hence it is only to be expected that, in some passages taken by themselves, he should seem to founder on one or other of these rocks. Any such passages, however, should surely be interpreted in the light of his main thesis, and while this thesis has perhaps been sufficiently indicated by citations already, it may be worth clinching the matter by quoting Hegel's own summary (§ 260) of his general view of the State: "The State is the realization of concrete freedom. But concrete freedom consists in this, that personal individuality and its particular interests not only attain their complete development and gain explicit recognition for their rights (in the family and the system of 'civil society'), but pass over of their own accord into devotion to universal interests. When that happens they know and will the universal . . . and are active in its pursuit. The result is that the universal does not prevail or attain perfection except along with the interests of individuals and through the cooperation of their knowledge and will. Individuals likewise do not live like private persons for their own ends alone but, in willing them, will the universal at the same time." How far Hegel succeeded in his endeavor to do justice to the rights of individuals is a matter for philosophic criticism; but any such criticism will misfire which, despite, e.g., the passage just quoted, maintains that in his view the individual is a mere means to the ends of the State.

"Prussianism" is associated not only with the suppression of conscience and individuality and the doctrine that might is right, but also with the glorification of war. Hegel's view on this subject is summarized by Mr. Carritt as follows: "War is justified on the grounds that by it domestic discontent and hankering after liberty are quelled and the inconsiderable nature of human happiness demonstrated by 'hussars with shining sabres.' "[26] What Hegel actually says is: "War is not to be regarded as an absolute evil"—the emphasis is on the word "absolute"—"or as a merely external accident resulting it may be from the injustice or the passions of nations or their rulers. . . . It is a matter of necessity that the finite, i.e., life and possessions, should be definitely established as something merely contingent, because the notion of the finite is the contingent. . . . Edifying sermons are preached about the vanity of temporal goods, but war is the state of affairs which makes us take this vanity in earnest. . . . Everyone thinks when he hears such sermons, however much he may be moved by them, that he will be able to preserve his own possessions. But if their insecurity is made a serious matter by hussars with shining sabres, then preaching turns into curses against the invader" (§ 324). It is true that Hegel goes on to affirm that peoples stagnate if they remain at peace and that war does result in the composing of domestic feuds, but his main point is that war is an unavoidable necessity. "In time of war," he continues, "right has lost its sway; might and chance rule." And yet "combatants regard it as a passing phase which ought not to be, and for this reason, even in war-time envoys are respected and war is not waged against private individuals or family life." "In modern times" (1820!) "war is humanely waged" (§ 338). In face of these quotations, can it be maintained either that Mr. Carritt's summary is fair or that Hegel is an apostle of frightfulness?

Finally, how does the teaching of the *Philosophie des Rechts* compare with the practice of Fascism and National-Socialism? So far as these ideologies make the unity of national life an ideal, Hegel is at one with them. In Italy the use of corporations in the organization of industry is strikingly reminiscent of his proposals, and the resemblance is doubtless not accidental. The relation between the *Deutsche Christen* and the German Government recalls Hegel's proposed partnership between Church and State. But it is only if half its doctrine is ignored that the *Philosophie des Rechts* can be interpreted as an apologia for the most criticized aspects of National-Socialism. Above all, where in the totalitarian State are his safeguards of "sub-

jective freedom'"? Where in his book is there any warrant for a
secret police? What would he have thought of the treatment of
the Jews? An answer to this question may be inferred from a
passage in the *Philosophie des Rechts* itself, where he says that
those who would exclude the Jews even from civil rights on the
ground of their race forget that the Jews are *men*, with the
rights of men, and that in fact experience has shown that thus
to exclude them is the worst of follies (second footnote to §
270).

NOTES

1. *Philosophical Theory of the State* (London, 1930), pp. 230 ff.
2. *German Philosophy and the War* (London, 1915).
3. *Les doctrines politiques des philosophes classiques de l'Allemagne* (Paris,
   1927), pp. 110 ff.
4. E.g., S. Hook: *From Hegel to Marx* (London, 1936), p. 19.
5. E.g., Aldous Huxley: *Ends and Means* (London, 1938), pp. 58, 171; E. A.
   Mowrer: *Germany Puts the Clock Back* (Penguin Books, London, 1938),
   pp. 38–39.
6. This is the work referred to in this article as the *Philosophie des Rechts.*
   The only English translation—*Hegel's Philosophy of Right,* by S. W. Dyde
   (London, 1896)—has long been out of print. A new translation, with
   commentary, by the writer of this article is in preparation. [Knox's fine
   translation of Hegel's *Philosophy of Right* was published in 1942.
   w. k.]
7. The letter is printed, with an introduction and notes by E. Crous (on which
   I have drawn for the facts about the Carlsbad decrees and the subsequent
   censorship), in Lasson's *Hegel-Archiv,* I, 2 (Leipzig, 1912), pp. 18 ff. This
   letter was first brought to my notice by Professor Sidney Hook of New
   York, whose kindness I acknowledge all the more readily in that I have
   come to different conclusions from his about Hegel's political objectivity.
8. *Hegel-Archiv,* I, 2, p. 57. (Here again the writer is indebted for the
   reference to Professor Hook.)
9. Copies were in Hegel's hands, however, before the end of 1820. See a letter
   to him (*Briefe von und an Hegel* (Leipzig, 1887), vol. ii, pp. 32–33), dated
   December 18, 1820, acknowledging a complimentary copy of the book.
10. By 1824 the censorship was considerably relaxed (Lenz: *Geschichte der
    Universität zu Berlin,* II, i—Halle, 1910—p. 183), but I cannot find that it
    was relaxed earlier, and I therefore assume that it was still rigid in 1821,
    and that Hegel's book was submitted and passed.
11. *Hegels Nürnberger Schriften,* hrsg. von J. Hoffmeister (Leipzig, 1938), p.
    470.
12. Eng. Tr. (London, 1929), vol. i, p. 63.
13. *Morals and Politics* (Oxford, 1935), p. 107.
14. *Proc. of Artis. Soc.,* 1935–6, p. 230.

15. Haym, who, in his *Hegel und seine Zeit* (1857), employs every available weapon to attack what he holds is Hegel's "servility" and conservatism, and makes much use of this preface, never mentions the sentence which I have been endeavoring to explain. Had he interpreted it in Mr. Carritt's sense, would he not undoubtedly have added it to his armory?

16. The evidence for this is quoted in a note by H. Falkenheim in Kuno Fischer: *Hegels Leben und Werke* (Heidelberg, 1911), p. 1232.

17. This faċt and those in the next paragraph for which I have quoted no reference are taken from an article by Dr. J. Hoffmeister in the *Geist der Gegenwart* supplement of the *Kölnische Zeitung* for December 12, 1937.

18. Rosenkranz: *Hegels Leben* (Berlin, 1844), p. 318.

19. *Hegel-Archiv*, I, 2, p. 21.

20. *Ibid.,* pp. 31–33.

21. These three are singled out for mention by Treitschke in his *Deutsche Geschichte im neunzehnten Jahrhundert* (Leipzig, 1919), vol. iii, p. 721. In what follows references in parentheses to numbered paragraphs are to the paragraphs of the *Philosophie des Rechts.*

22. In his Berlin lectures on the history of philosophy, Hegel says that Prussia is *auf Intelligenz gebaut.* This remark is doubtless to be explained in the light of the passage, in his *Philosophy of History,* treating Prussia as the embodiment of *Protestantism.*

23. *Morals and Politics,* p. 114. Citations could have been made from authors other than Mr. Carritt, but I take them from him because of recent English scholarly writings on Hegel his are probably the best known of those which adopt the point of view attacked in this article.

24. *Proc. of Arist. Soc.,* 1935–6, p. 236.

25. I am glad to find my argument here supported by a recent keen critic of Hegel—Mr. J. P. Plamenatz—in his *Consent, Freedom and Political Obligation* (Oxford, 1938), p. 33.

26. *Morals and Politics,* p. 108. [Cf. also Kaufmann's essay, section 11, below. W.K.]

2 *Reply*

E. F. CARRITT

In an article in the January number of *Philosophy* Professor Knox sets out to disprove "(i) that Hegel the man is justly accused of servility to the Prussian Government, and (ii) that there is any warrant in the text of his *Philosophie des Rechts* for the charge that Hegel the philosopher was an exponent of *Prussianism* and *frightfulness*."

In the course of this attempt he draws attention to two passages in which he thinks I misinterpreted Hegel in my *Morals and Politics.* (I) The first of these passages occurs on my p. 107 where I attribute to Hegel the view that 'the proper exercise of philosophy is in the service of the State.' The passage in the *Philosophie des Rechts* (Vorrede), after describing the views of an opponent as Rabulisterei der Willkür[a]

---

[a] "Pettifoggery of caprice" (Knox tr.). W.K.

reads: "Noch weniger ist sich *zu verwundern,* wenn die Regierungen auf solches Philosophiren endlich die Aufmerksamkeit gerichtet haben, da *ohnehin* bei uns die Philosophie nicht wie etwa bei den Griechen, als eine private Kunst exercirt wird, sondern sic eine öffentliche, das Publikum berührende Existenz, *vornehmlich oder allein* im Staatsdienste, hat."[b] (The italics throughout are mine.) Hegel goes on to say that hitherto the State, either through self-confidence or contempt, has left philosophical heresy free: "Weil sie nicht dazu kommt, die Substanz der Sachen zu berühren, ja nur zu ahnden; sie würde somit zunachst wenigstens polizeilich nichts gegen sich haben."[c] But, since the State "needs a deeper instruction and insight," and demands the satisfaction of this need from philosophy, it will not be influenced by any professional claims to freedom for the discussion of first principles, if these have a bearing upon conduct. (This looks very like the Athenian attitude to Socrates.)

Professor Knox then is concerned to show that these remarks are no evidence either that Hegel was servile to the Prussian Government or that he was an exponent of Prussianism.

In prosecuting the first of these attempts he points out several facts, given by Bosanquet, which I had forgotten. Hegel and the opponent, Fries, whom he abuses, were both, as university professors, civil servants in the pay of the Government, until Fries was dismissed, and were therefore perhaps bound either to refrain from criticizing it or to resign. The Government had recently decided to enforce a censorship upon academic publications. Hegel delayed the issue of his *Philosophie des Rechts,* but finally published it with a *Vorrede* explaining that, though

---

[b] "Still less is it a matter for surprise that governments have at last directed their attention to this kind of philosophy, since, apart from anything else, philosophy with us is not, as it was with the Greeks for instance, pursued in private like an art, but has an existence in the open, in contact with the public, and especially, or even only in the service of the state" (Knox tr.). w. K.

[c] "Because it fails to touch or even to guess at the substance of the things; no action, or at least no police action, would thus have been taken against it in the first instance . . ." (Knox tr.). W.K.

critical of the Government on some points, he "shared its opposition to revolutionary ideas."

All this has nothing to do with me. I did not use the word "servile," nor did I ever suggest that Hegel was moved by the mercenary desire to retain a job or to get a better one. I had overlooked that he was in Government pay and I could therefore consider that neither as an excuse nor an aggravation. I was shocked not that he simulated these views for money, but that he actually held them. I did imply that his reflection must have been distorted by party, social, or religious prejudices; just as Professor Knox and I might bring the same charge against one another without offense and almost certainly with some measure of truth. But that in *this* sense he was "servile" to the Prussian Government—that he was too ready to congratulate it upon the dismissal of a troublesome, if silly, professor and upon the tightening of an academic censorship—I still think. One can only read the passages.

Professor Knox argues that Hegel must really be deploring the oppression of the Prussian Government, because in the *Encyclopaedia* he ascribes philosophy to Absolute Mind which transcends Mind Objective where the State is placed. I agree that Hegel's metaphysic does not necessarily imply a repressive (or any other) policy. My contention precisely is that when he came to politics his prejudices led him to think this policy was so implied. Even if he had not made this particular remark, we could have guessed what his attitude would be from such sayings as "Der Staat ist also die Wirlichkeit des substantiellen Willens . . . das an und für sich Vernünftige. . . . Dieser Endzweck das höchste Recht gegen die Einzelnen hat, deren höchste Pflicht es ist, Mitglieder des Staats zu sein"[d] (*P.d.R.,* 258), and from his distinction between *Moralität* and *Naturrecht* in *Philosophie des Geistes,* § 502.

Nor did I use either the term frightfulness or Prussianism; but it might fairly be inferred that I thought Hegel's writings contained the germs which have been developed, with more or

[d] "As the actuality of the substantial will, the state is . . . that which is rational in and for itself" (my tr.). Carritt's *"also"* (thus) should be *"als"* (as). W.K.

less enthusiastic acknowledgment, by totalitarians of both Marxist and Fascist persuasions. I agree with Professor Knox that dismissal of professors and censorship of philosophy hardly come up to modern standards of frightfulness, but they might not unfairly be described as Prussianism or Russianism, though they are also practiced in places less subject to the limelight.

(2) A second alleged misinterpretation is a sentence on p. 108 of my *Morals and Politics:* "War is justified by Hegel on the grounds that by it domestic discontent and hankering after liberty are quelled and the inconsiderable nature of individual life and happiness demonstrated by 'hussars with shining sabres' " (*P.d.R.*, § 324).

Professor Knox quotes this passage, beginning: "War is not to be regarded as an absolute evil or as a merely external accident resulting, it may be, from the injustice or the passions of nations or their rulers" (he omits the words *überhaupt in solchem das nicht sein soll*).[e] He then proceeds: "It is true that Hegel goes on to affirm that people stagnate (!) if they remain at peace and that war does result in the composing of domestic feuds," but he insists that Hegel's emphasis is on the denial that war is an *absolute* evil, and finally asks: "In face of these quotations, can it be maintained either that Mr. Carritt's summary is fair or that Hegel is an apostle of frightfulness?" To the first question at least I think the answer of most readers would be: Yes. I do not know that I ever met anything which Hegel would call an "absolute" evil; such a thing is, I suppose, on his philosophy, impossible; certainly he could not so describe an immoral act. I take war to be an evil of the same kind as slavery or the vendetta, which we ought to try to remove. Hegel's defense of it, as educational, reminds me of those 'edifying sermons' (to quote his own sneer) which condemn attempts to discover cures for cancer or unemployment, on the ground that these are providentially designed as discipline for character. His defense of it as necessary reminds me

---

[e] "Generally, in what ought not to be" (my tr.). W.K.

of the nineteenth-century defense of child-labor. As to his denial that it presupposes any guilt, I agree with the criticism of T. H. Green:

"However widely distributed the agency may be which causes the destruction of life in war, it is still intentional human agency. The destruction is not the work of accident or nature. . . . The language indeed which we hear from the pulpit about war being a punishment for the sins of mankind is perfectly true, but it needs to be accompanied by the reminder that this punishment of the sin is simply a consequence of the sin and itself a further sin, brought about by the action of the sinner, not an external infliction brought about by agencies to which man is not a party" (*Political Obligation,* §§ 160–161).

When Guernica is bombed I am not edified. Nor could I comfortably tell my sons or pupils that it was not an absolute evil if by killing or being killed they should be strikingly reminded of mortality. Nor am I consoled by the romance of the "shining sabres." But Hegel's view that States have no duties to one another and that it is the highest duty of a State to promote its own power, against which other States have no right (*P.d.R.,* §§ 336, 337, 342–4), renders a justification of war inevitable, as personal "honor" justified dueling.

There remain three other instances of alleged misinterpretation, founded not on single passages, but rather on general impressions, and therefore to be discussed in a rather different way.

(i) "That by adopting Schiller's epigram, *Die Weltgeschichte ist das Weltgericht,* Hegel frankly identifies might with right" (*Morals and Politics,* p. 114).

(ii) That Hegel "defends the suppression of freedom of conscience" (i.e., I suppose of freedom of speech and of association).

(iii) That Hegel holds that "the individual is a mere means to the State's ends" (*Proc. of Arist. Soc.,* 1935–36, p. 236).

It is only the first and third of these misinterpretations of which I am accused, but I should like to say something shortly about all three. It is to be noticed that Professor Knox is prepared to maintain not only that these interpretations are unfair upon the whole, but that there are no "detailed passages" in Hegel to support them, though he agrees that they have often been given.

Against all these interpretations Professor Knox cites passages, with some of which I will try to deal before citing my own. But I should begin by disclaiming the belief that Hegel, any more than any other philosopher, was always consistent or that he was such a bad philosopher that *all* his inconsistencies were wrong. I cannot agree that "there is no warrant in the text of the *Philosophie des Rechts* for a charge that Hegel was an exponent of Prussianism and frightfulness," though I never made the charge. I am not sure if the wording here is meant to allow that such warrant *can* be found in the *Philosophie der Geschichte* and elsewhere. We are certainly entitled to interpret the former work by the latter, as Professor Knox relies upon the *Encylopädie* for his interpretation of the censorship passage. And since later we are told that "It is only if *half* its doctrine is ignored that the *Philosophie des Rechts* can be interpreted as an apologia for the most criticized aspects of National-Socialism," we may perhaps infer, without pledging ourselves to exact bisection, that (so far from there being no "detailed passages" to "warrant the charge"), it is only if we neglect the other half that we can avoid my interpretation.

(i) Taking then the first count: Did Hegel identify might with right? Professor Knox says: "What triumphs in history, Hegel thinks, is the right or God's purpose, the rightness of which is intrinsic to itself, not dependent on its might." Here I stand corrected. I ought not to have said that Hegel *identifies* might with right (in the sense that he does not distinguish them in thought), but only that he holds them inseparable, so that whatever we see prevailing, we can know, however wrong it appears, to be right. I think I might fairly have said that he identifies right causes with successful causes. Professor Knox cites as "plain words" which have been neglected: "Because sovereignty is the identity of all particular authorities, it easily gives rise to the common misconception, which mistakes it for sheer force (*Macht*), and identical with despotism" (*P.d.R.,* § 278). But the question is not whether all sovereigns, because they have power, are despots, but whether the power either of a sovereign or a despot is any evidence that he represents the will of God. And I find at least equally "plain" the words that "The existence of the State is the process of God upon earth" (*P.d.R.,* § 258),[f] and at least equally emphatic: "Die absolute Regierung . . . ist das unmittelbare Priesterthum des Allerhöchsten, in dessen Heiligthum sie mit ihm Rath pflegt und seine Offenbarungen erhält. Alles Menschliche und alle andere Sanction hört hier auf. . . . Jedes machen an ihr käme aus der Freiheit und dem Willen" (*System der Sittlichkeit,* p. 38).[g] Further on he explains his distinction between despotism, resting on mere physical strength (*Macht*), and *"Gewalt, reine entsetzliche Herrschaft . . . sie ist nothwending und gerecht insofern sie den Staat als dieses wirkliche Individuum* constituirt und erhält."[h] In the *Philosophie der Geschichte* (Lasson, viii, 2, p. 88) we read that the right of the *Weltgeist* is above everything that can be justified as excellent or noble; and the Weltgeist embodies itself in the State. And again, "What the absolute end of Spirit requires and accomplishes, what Providence does, transcends the moral obligations and responsibilities and the praise or blame of individuals. . . . The litany of private virtues, of moderation, of humility, of humanity, of mercy, must not be raised against supermen (*Welthistorische*)[i] and their deeds. World history may completely disre-

---

[f] This mistranslation is discussed at length in the Introduction, above, and so are two of the other quotations in this paragraph. w.k.

[g] "The absolute government . . . is the unmediated priesthood of the Most High in whose sanctuary it consults with him and receives his revelations. Everything human and all other sactions cease at this point. . . . All tinkering with it would issue from freedom and the will." See the preceding note. w.k.

[h] "Violence, pure terrible dominion . . . it is *necessary and just* insofar as it constitutes and preserves the state *as this actual individual.*" w.k.

[i] As it stands, this parenthesis makes little sense, but it is clearly meant to refer to "world-historical individuals." The overtones of "supermen"—a term Hegel did not use—are misleading. See note f above. For further discussion of world-historical individuals see the last essay, below, and my *Hegel,* sections 62 and 64. w.k.

gard the sphere of morality and the popular contrast of morality with politics" (Lasson, viii, 2, p. 153).

(ii)   These passages on success as the criterion of right have already provided some material for answering the second question: "Does Hegel repudiate freedom of conscience?" And we may also refer to the discussion of the censorship question at the beginning of this paper. Professor Knox on this point quotes the passage (*P.d.R.,* § 270, n. 2) where Hegel defends the Prussian toleration of Jews and Quakers even though the latter refuse military service. But in the same passage Hegel insists that they have thereby forfeited their citizenship and have, in that respect, been not inaptly compared to slaves. Professor Knox next quotes § 137 on conscience as a "sanctuary which it would be sacrilege to violate." But the whole passage reads: "Conscience, *as the union of subjective belief with the absolute* [i.e., the state] [j] is a sanctuary which it would be sacrilege to violate. But whether the conscience of any individual corresponds to this idea is a question . . . so *the state cannot recognize conscience in its individual form* of subjective conscience." A long section (*P.d.R.,* § 140), summarized in a paragraph of subsection (*e*), argues that, since judgments about duty are fallible, "to oppose the authority of my private conviction to law, which has the authority of God, of the state, and of centuries" is "a stupendous presumption." This implies that God's will is revealed to the state but not in conscience, which therefore the state must silence. This is explicit in the *Phil. d. Geschichte:* "The ethic (*Sittlickeit*) of the state is not of the reflective (*moralische*) kind where my conviction rules" (Lasson, p. 94).

(iii)   Does Hegel maintain that the individual is a mere means to the State?

(*a*)   Professor Knox's first argument is that Hegel allowed more freedom to the individual than Plato did. So modest a testimonial I would not contest, though others do. Indeed, I

---

[j] For Hegel the state is far from being "the absolute." It belongs to the sphere of objective spirit, while art, religion, and philosophy are the realms of absolute spirit. W.K.

should take Hegel's self-gratulation here as the sign of a lamentably low standard. It is hard to see how anybody not enslaved would have less freedom than Plato's workers. Nor must we forget that Hegel's own account of the *Bauernstand, der Stand der rohen Sittlichkeit* is as contemptuous as Plato's own (*System der Sittlichkeit,* pp. 30, 61, 65).

(b) Professor Knox then cites §§ 260 and 184 of the *P.d.R.* as asserting that "the modern state allows its subjects to develop to self-subsistent individuality." I would not deny that Hegel, like Burke, idealized the constitution of his own time and country as manifesting an almost perfect mean of liberty, which any reform would upset. But they only managed to do this by putting the golden mean at a very queer place in the scale. Hegel would allow individuals to "develop self-subsistently" so long as their well-being and *that of others* is subordinated to the well-being of the State as the State conceives it: *"Das Wohl eines Staats eine ganz andere Berechtigung hat als das Wohl des Einzelnen"* (*P.d.R.,* § 337).[k] "Allen Wert den der Mensch hat, alle geistige Wirklichkeit, hat er allein durch den Staat . . . So nur ist er in der Sitte." (*Phil. d. G.,* Lasson, viii, p. 90).[1] "Der Staat ist nicht um der Bürger willen da; man könnte sagen, er ist der Zweck, und sie sind seine Werkzeuge (Indes ist dies Verhältniss von Zweck und Mittel hier nicht passend)."[m]

No doubt Hegel professed (as who does not?) and even persuaded himself (as who cannot?) that he was an admirer of freedom. And he managed this by giving the word a peculiar meaning of his own. Freedom is not the power of doing what you like (*P.d.R.,* § 15) nor what you think right (§ 140). He holds that those and only those are free who desire above all

---

k "The welfare of a state has claims to recognition totally different from those of the welfare of the individual" (Knox tr.). W.K.

1 "All of the value of a human being, all of his spiritual actuality [or realization] he achieves only through the state . . . only thus does he become ethical. . . ." W.K.

m "The state does not exist for the sake of the citizens; one might say that it is the purpose and they are its instruments (but any such relation of means and ends is altogether inappropriate here)" (*Ibid.,* 91). W.K.

things to serve the success and glory of their State. In desiring this they are desiring that the will of God should be done, since "dass der Staat ist, ist der Gang Gottes in der Welt."[n] So there is no conflict between their subjective goodness or freedom and objective goodness or freedom; what they want to do is what the State enforces and what ought to be done. If an individual believes he ought to do what is not for the success and glory of his State, he must be "forced to be free," though we may contemptuously approve his "blosse Moralität."[o] If he asks how he is to know that the rulers' idea of success and glory, or of the means to them, is correct, that the *de facto* State is also *de jure*, ακριβεῖ λόγω κρειττων,[p] the answer must surely be that the very fact of their being rulers is the surest sign of God's will that they should be. This must be the answer, since Hegel contends that supermen[q] like Caesar, who in disobeying the State for private ends, were strong enough to succeed, are "justified," however we may condemn them from the point of view of *Moralität*. If they fail they are condemned. Right without might is "blosses Sollen."[r] What happens to this freedom when the *Weltgeist* transfers its patronage to some other State, so that ours has no longer the "mission" to be glorious and successful, seems doubtful. Our defeat proves that God has abandoned us. Ought we to fight against him? It is the mission of the dominant State to sink our leaky ship, and logically we ought to rat. We shall then be free because our desires conform to the will of God, which can only be conjectured by what it brings about. Sibree's translation of K. Hegel's edition of the *Philosophie der Geschichte* (to which I have not had access) contains a passage, which I do not find in either Gans or Lasson: "Every Englishman will say: We are the men who

[n] See note f above. W.K.

[o] "Mere *Moralität*." For some discussion of the genesis of Hegel's sharp distinction between *Moralität* and *Sittlichkeit*, see section 21 of my *Hegel*. W.K.

[p] The point of the Greek phrase, marred by several errors in the original, is not altogether clear. It may be an inexact echo of Plato's *Republic*, 340E, and the intended meaning might be: "Stronger by definition." W.K.

[q] Hegel did not use the term "supermen." W.K.

[r] "Mere ought." W.K.

navigate the ocean and have the commerce of the world, to whom the East Indies belong and their riches; . . . A nation is moral, virtuous and vigorous so long as it realizes its great aims" (p. 77). This only amplifies *Philosophie des Rechts,* § 347, "The nation to whom such a mission is entrusted by the World-spirit is, for its epoch, supreme. Against this, its absolute right, the spirits of other nations have no rights whatever."

The passages on which I would mainly rely for this general impression of Hegel's political philosophy are (*a*) for internal policy § 258 of the *Philosophie des Rechts,* which I summarized in my *Morals and Politics,* pp. 105–7 (*b*) for external policy, the Introduction to the *Philosophie der Geschichte.* These two works are translated severally by Dyde and Sibree.

Finally, if this, my general interpretation of Hegel's political theory, is wrong, it has at least the excuse of being shared by many of his most admiring and able exponents.

(*a*) H. von Treitschke is commonly considered as the theoretical protagonist of German State-idolatry and militarism. In his *Politik* (of which selections are translated by H. W. C. Davis in *Political Thought of H. von Treitschke*) he clearly regards himself as a disciple and popularizer of Hegel, his chief criticism being that the master, for instance in questions of religion, was too totalitarian. He regards it as the *reductio ad absurdum* of democracy that it should logically disregard even distinctions of race. "It is materialism that rejects war" (*op. cit.,* pp. 182, 153).

(*b*) W. Wallace (*Hegel's Philosophy of Mind,* clxxxi-iii) summarizes Hegel thus: "It is foolish to oppose the interest or (as it is expressed by the more morally obnoxious word) the utility of the state to its right; . . . war (which some would fain abolish or moralize) has to decide not which of the rights asserted by either party is the true right (for both parties have a true right) but which right has to give way to the other. . . . All states are founded by the sublime force of great men. . . . The state is the self-certain absolute mind, which recognizes no definite authority but its own; which acknowledges no abstract rules of good and bad, shameful and mean, craft and deception." Wallace comments: "It is evident from these propositions that Hegel takes that view of political supremacy which has been associated with the name of Hobbes . . . so also Hobbes describes the prerogatives of the sovereign Leviathan. . . . The absolute government is divine, self-sanctioned, and not made. . . . If we ask, where does this public opinion appear? . . . Hegel answers, it is embodied in the Aged and the Priests. . . ."

(c) T. H. Green (*Freedom in Morality*, § 6) says: "We cannot significantly speak of freedom except with reference to individual persons; only in them can freedom be realised; therefore the realisation of freedom in the state can only mean the attainment of freedom by individuals through influences which the state supplies. . . . What Hegel says of the state in this respect seems hard to square with facts. . . . Hegel's account of freedom as realised in the state does not seem to correspond to the facts of society as it is, or even as, under the unalterable conditions of human nature, it ever could be."

(d) F. H. Bradley (*Ethical Studies*, "My Station and its Duties"); after referring to Hegel, says, "Virtue is not a troubling oneself about a peculiar and isolated morality of one's own. The striving for a positive morality of one's own is futile and in its very nature impossible of attainment; in respect of morality the saying of the wisest men of antiquity is true, that to be moral is to live in accordance with the moral tradition of one's country."

(e) D. H. Ritchie, who in his *Rationality of History* (*Essays in Philosophical Criticism*, ed. Seth and Haldane) was a whole-Hegelian, says: "In a sense, might is right. If individuals or nations are able permanently to succeed in influencing the world, we must regard their conduct as justified by their success. . . . The permanence of any 'counsel or work' is the test of its divine sanction" (p. 140) (*Die Weltgeschichte ist das Weltgericht!*).

(f) Bosanquet, who defends Hegel on the same lines as Professor Knox, asserts that "the state *de facto* is also the state *de jure*" (*Philosophical Theory of the State*, p. 185) and that "in submitting even to forcible restraint, when imposed by

society in the true common interest, I am obeying only myself"
(p. 107); though he admits that to call his "freedom" is "more
or less a metaphor." A "modern state" is "the typical mind, the
very essence of reason" (p. 281). "The general will must be
the rational will even though people are not aware of it" (p.
240). "The state is the guardian of the whole moral world, but
not a factor within an organized moral world. Moral relations
presuppose an organized life, but such a life is only within the
state, not in relations between the state and other communities" (p. 325). "If the act was immoral, can the state as such
really have willed it?" (p. 323). To justify all this Bosanquet
puts forward the quite Hegelian, but for political theory aston-
ishing, view that the distinction of persons is the same as that
of faculties or interests in myself, so that there is no more
injustice in developing one man at the expense of others than
in sacrificing, say, my athletics to my philosophy. "The true
particularisation of the human universal does not necessarily
coincide with the distinction between different persons. . . . The
stress seems therefore to lie in the attainment of the true
particularisation which does justice to the maximum of human
capacity, rather than on the mere relations which arise between
the members of a *de facto* plurality" (pp. 170-179). This,
which would justify slavery, seems so outrageous that I should
have thought I must have misunderstood it were it not in
complete agreement with Hegel's doctrine of the "inconsiderable" nature of individuality and Bosanquet's own formulation
that "the world of claims and counterclaims" is an illusion.

(*g*) In the same spirit Professor Lord (*Principles of Politics,* 1921) writes: "The merely factual difference between
individual minds or their acts is in itself quite insignificant and
meaningless" (p. 270)—so you can punish me for your crime!

(*h*) Professor Reyburn (*Hegel's Ethical Theory,* 1921)
says, "Moral responsibility is an abstraction" (p. 195).

(*i*) Professor Sabine in his admirably fair *History of Political Theory,* 1937 (pp. 635-639), says: "Hegel continually
identified right and force, partly because he imputed to nature

an ideal constitution that inevitably gives the greatest power to right, and partly because he regarded might as making right. . . . The state is continually represented as standing for the highest possible ethical value. . . . Hegel was at times led to the . . . conclusion that a good citizen need do nothing but conform to the existing state of affairs in his society. It was characteristic of him that he repeatedly equated individual choice with mere caprice, sentimentality and fanaticism. Again and again he branded the right of private judgment as a merely 'superficial' theory." [8]

These few quotations must serve to show that for eighty years Hegel has commonly been interpreted by his most favorable critics in a "totalitarian" sense—in the sense that he thinks might indicates right; that he defends the suppression of free-speech and the subordination of conscience to law and tradition; that he thinks war necessary and the attempt to abolish it silly; that he believes that state to have some other justification than the welfare of its members or the enforcement of justice, but to have no duties to other states. That he ascribed any value to the democratic principles of equality and of representative government, I suppose, Professor Knox would not suggest.

---

[8] Like some of Carritt's other quotations, these quotations are inexact. Moreover, Sabine said in his Preface to the Second Edition, which is dated December 19, 1949: "The chapters from Hegel to the end of the book . . . have been completely rewritten. . . . The author now believes that the connection made in the first edition between national socialism and the Hegelian theory of the state was hasty and superficial. For this change of view he should express his indebtedness to analyses of national socialism and Hegelianism by German critics, especially to Herbert Marcuse's *Reason and Revolution*. . . ." W.K.

3 *Rebuttal*

T. M. KNOX

In the course of his reply, in the April issue of *Philosophy,* to my article on "Hegel and Prussianism," which appeared in the January number, Mr. Carritt says that for his general impression of Hegel's political philosophy, so far as the internal policy of the State is concerned, he relies mainly on § 258 of the *Philosophie des Rechts.* In that paragraph we are told, *inter alia,* that the State is absolutely rational; in the *Anmerkung* which follows, Hegel explains that rationality consists in the thoroughgoing unity of universal and individual, or, more concretely, in the unity of objective freedom with subjective freedom (i.e., the individual's freedom to know and will his private ends). It follows from Hegel's remarks that individual freedom and private welfare are in his view integral elements in the rational State to which he says it is the individual's highest duty to belong. (Compare the *Zusatz* to § 265, where he says that the end of the State is the happiness of the citizens, and that the State's footing is insecure if it is not the means of satisfying subjective aims.) In face, therefore, of Hegel's own exegesis of this paragraph, which Mr. Carritt regards as crucial, I find it hard to understand how he can still hold that Hegel believes the individual to be a mere means to the State's ends (see pp. 37ff., above).

To one who reads the *Philosophie des Rechts* as a whole and does not rely on isolated passages, the tenor of Hegel's view of the State is not really in doubt. He believes that the essence of the nation State is a tension between the State's power on the one side and the individual's freedom on the other. If the tension is destroyed by laying exclusive emphasis on the latter, the result is anarchy and the disappearance of the State; if by laying emphasis exclusively on the former, then the State becomes "mere might and a synonym for despotism" (§ 278). As I indicated in my article, it is open to a critic to consider Hegel's safeguards for private freedom and to maintain that they are insufficient; what perplexes me is criticism like Mr. Carritt's, which ignores these safeguards, implies that they do not exist, and consequently misses what for Hegel is the very essence of the State, namely the tension to which I have referred.

Mr. Carritt concludes his reply by summarizing an interpretation of Hegel which he claims has been current for eighty years, and to which he seems to subscribe. I should like to make some comments on his summary—a summary which I do not believe those whom he quotes would accept.

(i) "Hegel thinks that might indicates right." This is certainly an overstatement, if not actually false. Hegel believes that right is mighty, but that is not what Mr. Carritt says. If he had believed that "might indicates right" there would have been no sense in his clear distinction between brute force and the "might of the Idea" (see, e.g., footnote to § 258) and his repudiation of despotism (e.g., *Anmerkung* to § 278).

(ii) "Hegel defends the suppression of free speech." Here again we have an overstatement. Hegel defended the dismissal of Fries, but he also advocated free speech and the freedom of the press (§ 319). A critic here is entitled to say that the freedom advocated is too circumscribed, or is allowed for the wrong reasons; but I do not see why § 319, and not the remark about Fries in the Preface, is to be dismissed as an "inconsistency." This is the line which Mr. Carritt appears to take (see p. 37, above); but to dismiss either of Hegel's strains of thought as an "inconsistency" is to miss the whole point of his doctrine (see above, my second paragraph).

(iii) "Hegel defends the subordination of conscience to law and tradition." This is true, but it is misleading as it stands. Hegel's doctrine is that while conscientiousness is intrinsic to concrete morality (*Sittlichkeit*), it is only its form; to be justified, it must be conviction of what is objectively right (§ 141). Conscientious conviction alone (mere *Moralität*, abstract morality) is no excuse for murder (§ 140). With the question of whether Hegel is right or wrong here, I am not at present concerned, but it would be interesting to know how many of those who, with Hegel, allow conscientious objections to military service, will go on, against him, to allow immunity and moral justification, on the strength of conscientious convictions, to conscientious murderers and sadists.

(iv) "Hegel thinks war necessary and the attempt to abolish it silly." To this assertion I raise no objections; but it is not the same as what Mr. Carritt wrote in *Morals and Politics,* and now still defends (p. 33f., above) as a fair summary of Hegel's view. I notice, however that in criticizing what I said in my article on this topic, he still leaves unmentioned the most crucial parts of the quotation from Hegel which I used to criticize him.

(v) "Hegel believes the State to have some other justification than the welfare of its members or the enforcement of justice." This also is true; though it would be fair to point out that Hegel believes that the State does secure both of these things incidentally, even though securing them is not its essence.

(vi) "Hegel believes the State to have no duties to other States." I do not know whether this is true or not. Hegel's statements conflict, and I am not prepared to reject either of them as an "inconsistency." He says that the State's final law is its own interest, and implies that it may override and break its obligations to other States. On the other hand, he also says that "treaties ought to be kept, that envoys ought to be respected, that war ought not to be waged against domestic institutions," and so forth, and this clearly implies that the State *has* duties to other States.

(vii) Mr. Carritt thinks that I will not suggest that Hegel ascribed any value to the "democratic principles of equality and representative government." Whether Hegel's remarks about inequality in § 200 and the special characteristics which he ascribes to the members of the Upper House (§§ 305–307) are tantamount to a rejection of the "democratic principle of equality," I do not know, and I will make no suggestion with regard to that. But I am prepared to suggest that Hegel attached great importance to representative government. A Lower House of Parliament, representative of each of the main branches of civil society, is an integral and essential part of Hegel's proposed constitution. But since it is one of his chief safeguards for private freedom I cannot feel surprise that Mr. Carritt allows it no importance.

Finally, I took exception to Mr. Carritt's attribution to Hegel of the view that "philosophy's proper exercise is in the service of the State." Mr. Carritt alludes to my criticism at some length, but he says nothing of its essence, namely my attempt to show that the words which he quotes from Hegel mean no more than that professors of philosophy in Prussia were civil servants.

4 *Final Rejoinder*

E. F. CARRITT

As the discussion is now to be closed, let me say that I have profited by it, and now have an impression of Hegel's political theory as less consistent than before. I hope Professor Knox can return the compliment. I will take his main points briefly in order.

In *P.d.R.*, § 258, Hegel certainly says "the State" is absolutely rational. And who can question that to a State we know to be absolutely rational, just, and beneficent we owe implicit obedience? But he goes on to say that "*Every* modern State, whatever faults we may recognize in it, if it is a developed modern State, has the essential characteristics of a State," i.e., I suppose, the rationality which invariably obliges us to implicit obedience. I find this a hard doctrine about the Prussia or Britain of 1820 or today. The vacillation between the ideal and the actual is of course crucial for the whole discussion. In

Hegel's rational State, where "subjective" and "objective freedom" are identified, the "coercive State" would have "withered
away." But it is only in our own coercive States that the
problems of obedience, reform, and resistance arise. I feel
vague about the meaning of the word "tension" in this context.
Does it imply hostility and struggle, or a harmony of balance?
Anyhow it is obvious that in any actual State there must be
some freedom (since not every detail can be prescribed), but
also *some* discipline, and therefore not that complete union of
subjective and objective freedom which obliges to unquestion-
ing obedience. I dealt with § 278 in April. I agree with § 265,
and wish I could make it consistent with the passages I then
quoted (pp. 36-37, above).

The numbering of the following points is Professor Knox's:

(i) Agreeing that Hegel thinks right always has might, he
denies that it follows that might always has right. "Mighty" is a
relative term, and I cannot believe that Hegel meant that,
though right has always a little might, it sometimes has less
than wrong has. From the *P.d. Geschichte* (where "immoral"
acts are "justified" by success) he clearly thinks that, in the
fairly long run, what succeeds is always right. Or would Professor Knox say that only in "ideal States" (condemned in *P.d.R.
Vorrede*, p. 18) is the idea realized?

I take the distinction between "brute force" and "the might
of the Idea" to be that the might of the latter, being more
"cunning," succeeds in the end.

(ii) On once more rereading *P.d.R. Vorrede* I still think
Hegel not only alludes to the fact that Prussian professors
(lucky Schopenhauer!)[a] were civil servants, but approves of
that system and of the Government's action in dismissing an
opposition professor and tightening an existing academic censorship. In § 319 Hegel refuses to define freedom of speech as
"being allowed to say what you please," and clearly means by
it "being allowed to say what you ought to be allowed," i.e., a
"union of subjective and objective freedom." It is therefore

---

[a] Schopenhauer never became a professor—but he tried. For the details, see
section 54 of Kaufmann's *Hegel*. W.K.

easy for him to say that *this* freedom of speech ought to be, and the real question: "How much saying what you please is consistent with the freedom of other people in other respects or with their other rights?" does not arise.

(iii) I agree that conscientious convictions about military or other killing may be wrong, and that, when we are convinced they are, we may think it our duty to "punish" the resulting actions in the interest of the freedom of others. My protest is against the doctrine, which Professor Knox agrees to be Hegel's, that we always ought "to submit our conscience to law and tradition" as if the makers of these were certainly infallible and disinterested. The same claim has been as reasonably made for Church Councils (of various churches) and for the Third International, only they have less might.

(iv) Professor Knox agrees that Hegel thinks war is necessary, and the attempts to prevent it silly, and that it does not arise from injustice or passion, but may be commended as quieting internal discontent. But still he does not think my summary of the doctrine in *Morals and Politics,* p. 108, or *Philosophy* (see pp. 33-34, above), fair. I only ask that these passages should be read with his criticism in *Philosophy* (see pp. 26-27, above). The exculpatory passage I am blamed for neglecting says that wars end, grow humaner, and respect ambassadors and private persons. It needs no comment.

(v) He admits that Hegel's essential justification of the State is neither that it secures the welfare of its members, nor that it enforces justice. Yet he objects to my saying that this makes the "inconsiderable" subjects a means to the State, as seems to be admitted in the passage I quoted.

(vi) He does not know whether or not "Hegel believes the State to have no duties to other States" because Hegel's "statements conflict." Yet he does not admit these conflicting statements are inconsistent. I do not follow this.

(vii) I am not sure how far Hegel's Lower House, which seems to have a "corporative" character, is only "virtually" representative in the sense dear to Whig oligarchies, but in the *System d. Sittlichkeit,* III, iii, he thinks that the sanctity of a ruling class would be diminished if it were elected.

In view, then, of admittedly "conflicting statements," what is Hegel's fundamental teaching? Perhaps the difference between Professor Knox and myself partly depends on his exclusive use of the *P.d.R.*, while I had interpreted it by help of the *P. d. Geschichte* and *System der Sittlichkeit*. But I thought the only answer, other than a bare statement of impression, was to note the interpretations given by qualified and especially by favorable critics. Since my April article I have happened upon two more, which are significant:

(1) Professor Vaughan, who (paradoxically enough, as I think) admires Hegel more than any other political philosopher, is yet constrained, in his *Studies in the History of Political Philosophy,* to say: "The memory of Fichte and Hegel is for ever burdened with the theory of the 'absolute state,' to which Bismarck harnessed the principle of nationality. . . . Before the 'stark congealment of blood and iron, in which their theories have resulted, even Fichte and Hegel, it may be hoped in charity, would have stood aghast' " (I 3). "Hegel, followed by a select band of English writers, identifies 'liberty' with the Prussian constitution" (268). "Fichte and Hegel . . . destroy that principle of individuality . . . without which the unity of the state sinks into a mere mechanical conformity. . . . In exposing the abuses inherent in the present distribution of property . . . they can claim no part" (II 5*). "Hegel, the theorist and idolater of Prussian bureaucracy" (96). "Nobody could be readier, when it suited his purpose . . . to assure the world that the most retrograde and oppressive institutions, being undeniably actual, must also be accepted as indisputably rational" (295). Paraphrasing *Philosophie der Geschichte,* pp. 25–33, he says: "Men's passions lie closer to them than the *artificial* and tedious discipline of self-restraint, morality and right" (289; my italics).

(2) Professor Gilson in *The Unity of Philosophical Experience* says: " (Hegel's dialectical justifications of war) are really and truly murderous ideas, and all the blood for which they are responsible has not yet been shed. Yet they are the last word of Hegelianism" (p. 252); and "When Fascism got the upper hand in Italy, Gentile's Hegelianism was fully justified in

welcoming it in the name of Hegel's theory of the state. . . . By saying that the state asserts its own autonomy in war, Gentile was merely repeating what we have seen to be the authentic Hegelian conception of the state" (294).

Professor Knox in his reply to Mr. J. A. Spender in the April number of *Philosophy* justifies his contention (in the previous number) that Hegel does not teach that success justifies immorality, as follows: "*If you like,* Hegel holds, you *may* judge that the great man is proud, immoral, heartless, and cruel, but these moral judgments are irrelevant [to what?] because they apply only to the overt [= inward?] character of the great man's deed and not at all to the substance of what he effects. For instance, Caesar's opponents had the *law and constitution* on their side, and his advance to autocracy was therefore *technically* unjust and wrong, but the foundation of the Roman Empire was an advance in civilization. Hegel further holds that at times *before constitutional law is established,* the great man has no option but to resort to force and violence, in order to establish law and order. Once a rational, i.e., a free, constitution is established, the right to use force has gone and changes must be brought about by constitutional means. Many writers have held that moral judgments are out of place in historical writing." (Italics and words in brackets are mine.)

Surely there are inconsistencies here. First we seem to be told that all Hegel meant was the stale platitude that a *bad act* may have good or felicific results. Then we are told that what he meant was that the alleged "bad" acts were only illegal, but *morally good.* Then we hear that once law and constitutions are established, force (and therefore Caesar's force) is *wrong.* Finally we are told that the whole discussion is considered by many writers nonsensical since moral judgments are out of place, i.e., I suppose must not be made about the past.

But Hegel is passing moral judgments. He is maintaining that *Sittlichkeit* is superior to *Moralität*; that the action of Caesar was immoral and yet *gerecht;* that States have the *duty* to aggrandize themselves at the cost of weaker neighbors (*Philosophie des Rechts,* § 258, *Philosophie der Geschichte,* Introduction).

II The Second Debate

The Second Doctor

5 *Hegel Rehabilitated?*

SIDNEY HOOK

      The English translation of Hegel's political writings provides an opportunity to re-examine certain conventional assessments of his social and political philosophy. Around few figures in the history of thought have the winds of controversy blown so fiercely. Ever since the first World War, Anglo-American idealistic philosophy seems to have been embarrassed by its Hegelian heritage. One could argue, however, with some plausibility that thinkers as diverse as Royce, Bradley, and McTaggart brought more to the Hegelian tradition than they received from it. On key points, especially in their refusal to accept the dialectical hanky-panky about the law of contradiction, they diverge sufficiently from Hegel to make it questionable whether it is just to consider them merely

The following four papers originally appeared in *Encounter* (England), January and November 1965 and March and May 1966.

disciples. Nonetheless, the drift of their social and religious views was similar enough to bring them under suspicion of ideological complicity. Actually, absolute idealism was brought down with the weapons of logical analysis; but the zest with which they were wielded testified to the presence of more than philosophical passion.

The reaction against chauvinism, reinforced by the growth of pacifism in the period between the two world wars, led to a respite from over-simple political explanations of social and cultural phenomena. But with the rise of Hitlerism and the outbreak of World War II, hostility to Hegel—as well as to Nietzsche—flared up with greater intensity. Yet whatever their intellectual sins neither one was a racialist. Although Hegel had glorified the State and sung the uses of war (at a time when most armies were largely professional), his emphasis on Reason made the Nazis uneasy. It smacked of something Jewish. Besides, he was an acknowledged intellectual ancestor of Marx. Outside of Germany (except among German refugee intellectual circles brooding over their cultural past) this coolness of the Nazis toward Hegel went unobserved. Every philosophically semi-literate leader writer had a field day excoriating Hegel and/or Nietzsche for the baneful influence of their Statism and Might-Makes-Right doctrine on events.

The fiercest attack on Hegel from the ranks of the professional philosophers is Karl Popper's diatribe against him in *The Open Society*. Its virulence matches that of Schopenhauer's and is based on as careful and sympathetic study of Hegel's writings. Popper did not have to consult a solicitor to see how far he could go in abusing Hegel without running afoul of the law.

In Marxist circles Hegel was never held responsible for German militarism or Fascism. This was an *a priori* judgment and not reached by a critical study of texts or intellectual history. It was derived from the assumption that since Marx took his theoretical point of departure from Hegel, the latter represented, by definition, the highest point of development of bourgeois society. And as Fascism in all its varieties was the ideology of "bourgeois society in decline," it could not be laid at Hegel's door. The treatment of Hegel among Bolshevik-Leninists has always been respectful except for a period when Stalin and Kaganovich fancied themselves philosophers. Among the reasons for purging Deborin in the early thirties as a "menshevising idealist" was that he concerned himself too much with the problems of the Hegelian dialectic and not enough with the role of philosophy in the Five-Year Plan. Today, Hegel's philosophical stock has never been higher among Communist philosophers. He is receiving credit not only for his method but for anticipating in some respects Marx's criticism of bourgeois society and the phenomenon of human alienation.

It was to be expected that in time the harsh and unjust judgment of Popper and others would be challenged. As is usual in such matters, the reaction has swung to the opposite extreme. Hegel is being rapidly rehabilitated not only in Germany and France (in Italy he never really was eclipsed, despite Croce who remained an Hegelian *malgré lui*) but also in the English-speaking world. The long introductory essay by Dr. Z. A. Pelczynski which prefaces the excellent translation by T. M. Knox, to whom we are already in debt for his rendering of *The Philosophy of Law,* [a] is an unabashed attempt to picture a new Hegel for our times. Far from being a reactionary or totalitarian thinker, we are asked to believe that he is not even a conservative or authoritarian one! Hegel emerges from the treatment at Dr. Pelczynski's eager and competent hands washed clean as a constitutional liberal, almost a democrat, one of the great figures in "the main stream of Western European political theory"—whose chief currents are "constitutionalism, democracy, and progress." Although Mr. John Plamenatz does not go so far as this in the illuminating and careful chapter on Hegel in his recent *Man and Society,* he, too, expresses surprise at discovering that Hegel is not as reactionary as has been commonly assumed.

[a] I.e., *Hegel's Philosophy of Right.* w.k.

Hegel's *Political Writings* by themselves have little intrinsic philosophical interest. Were they not written by Hegel, they would be ignored despite their comparative readability and, in places, their nervous, jaunty style. But they are of the first importance in determining how to read, how to decipher, how to get at the extra-philosophical motivation of a thinker of whom Friedrich Tönnies despairingly complained: *"Sein Wesen war Zweideutigkeit—er kannte so, er kannte auch anders."* [b] One of the expressions frequently encountered in expositions of Hegel is "his secret." Why should Hegel's "secret" be so hard to fathom?

From the point of view of pure logic, it is easy to square any nonempirical metaphysical system with any political position whatsoever. This makes it possible for Thomists to profess belief in democracy and for Hegelians to advocate radical republicanism. But it is not pure logic that determines which ideas will become the rallying cry of a social movement but their possible use in furthering interests in a specific historical context. And this use is derived from *attitudes* which certain large ideas express and encourage rather than from the propositions they strictly imply. That is why formal contradictions in professed doctrine are not an embarrassment to a social movement. Bertrand Russell somewhere says that a philosopher's inconsistencies are the clue to his passions (and this applies to him no less aptly than to others). If we extend this *bon mot* to a philosopher's systematic ambiguities, they may point to "the secret" of the Hegelian system. The political writings of Hegel, most of them unpublished in his lifetime, make it easier to check our hypothesis of Hegel's intent.

Were it not for Dr. Pelczynski's learned introduction to Hegel's *Political Writings,* I would have said that they make unmistakably plain not only the motivation behind his social

---

[b] *Kannte* (knew by acquaintance) is grammatically impossible. Hook surely means *konnte,* although the quotation does not make very much sense in any case: "Ambiguity was of his essence: he could do things this way, he also could do them that way." W.K.

and political philosophy but behind his logic and metaphysics as well. This has no bearing upon their validity, but it does help us in making out what Hegel is trying to say and in explaining some curious discrepancies in his position.

I want to state what I believe Hegel's motivation to be and what evoked it before examining Dr. Pelczynski's interpretation. Hegel's manuscript on the *Constitution of Germany* (written between 1799 and 1802) reveals him as an ardent nationalist fired with a desire to see the emergence of Germany as a powerful unified state under the forceful personality of a modern Theseus. The primary task of the monarch, after forging national unity, would be to liberate Germany from the domination and fear of revolutionary France (the left bank of the Rhine had been lost at the Congress of Rastadt), and bring to an end the long record of German humiliation. In short, Hegel was a German patriot and nationalist from the very *beginning* of his career, and before his philosophical system took shape; he did not first become one (as Plamenatz asserts) after the fall of Napoleon.

In Hegel's view the deplorable state in which Germany found herself was attributable chiefly to two things. The first was the traditional love of independence of the German states, allegedly rooted in the stubbornness and waywardness of the German character itself. The German states clung to their feudal privileges despite changing times and conditions. This historical individualism with its emphasis on ancient writs as the source of present rights Hegel regards as the essence of reaction. When he criticizes the "positivity" of law he means the charter of ancient rights and privileges which legitimize institutions that are overripe to the point of rottenness. He does *not* mean, as Herbert Marcuse suggests in his *Reason and Revolution: Hegel and the Rise of Social Theory,* "positivism." Hegel opposed positivism on other grounds as a form of empiricism.

The second cause of German collapse was the event or series of events whose consequences had exposed the fact that Germany was no longer a state, that she lacked the national solidarity and public authority essential to the existence of a state. The French revolutionary invasions, inspired by a false conception of freedom, had laid waste the German country-side. The war against Germany was not the result of a desire for pillage but of the French abstract conception of freedom. At one place it is referred to as "French libertarian madness." This clamor for freedom had infected the Germans, too, but they had been sobered by the grim experience of war.

> It is clear that as a result of ten years of war [1792–1802] and the misery of a large part of Europe, so much has been learnt, at least in theory, to make us more inaccessible to a blind clamour for freedom. In this bloody game the cloud of freedom had evaporated: in trying to embrace the cloud, the nations have flung themselves into an abyss of misery. . . .

Hegel's social and political philosophy, only adumbrated in these writings, but elaborated in his published work, was designed to overcome both misconceptions of freedom. It undercut, on the one hand, the German particularistic notion expressed in the desire to be left alone, to cling to outworn rights to the absurd lengths of acceptance of the slogan *Fiat justitia pereat Germania*—and on the other, the abstract French universalist demands whose stress on equality led to the terrorism of reason. These dangerous ideas were attractive to some German patriots who felt that they had a mass appeal which could strengthen resistance to French aggression. Hegel refused to surrender the term "freedom" to either side. It was necessary only to reinterpret it. That society was truly free, according to Hegel, in which all groups are subordinated to the State, in which important political decisions are made, after consultation with qualified representatives (not necessarily elected) of different social groups, by an absolute ruler resting on a permanent bureaucracy of trained officials. Democracy is the rule of the mob. Whatever social changes are necessary would be introduced *from above* with proper attention to the people's readiness for them. The sheep must not be sheared out of season. The greatest of all dangers to a truly free society emanates from the abstract demand for equality. It finds its "logical" expression in the guillotine which vainly tries to make people equal by cutting off their heads. It can succeed only in making people equal in death. In life and society there are different ways of being equal. Fanaticism, unable to understand and accept the virtues of hierarchy, is the enemy.

In his essays, "The Proceedings of the Estates Assembly in Würtemberg" and "The English Reform Bill," Hegel spells out in shrewd detail his conception of the well-ordered society. He condemns universal suffrage as opening the doors to "democratic formlessness" and "chance." The "fitness of the electors" must be guaranteed by certain qualifications imposed on them, and even so they will never be as trustworthy as public officials. The "will of the people"? A "great word"! But "what is one's true and real will?" Hegel's answer is: "what is good for one." It follows that if the representatives or government know what is good for the people, they are expressing the people's "true and real will" no matter what the people themselves actually want to choose. (Where have we heard this ominous line before?)

The Estates elected by the qualified voters, who constitute a comparative handful of the population, have the right to make legislative proposals and to criticize proposals laid before them but—crucial point!—they do not have absolute power of the purse over the monarch who must be allowed independent means raised by taxation or otherwise. No legislation by the Estates can be validly enacted into law unless the monarch approves. The monarch has the right to initiate legislation.

It is unnecessary to go into further detail and trace the differences between the position taken in these political writings and in the *Philosophy of Right*. Enough has been said to indicate that for Hegel, Bismarck's Germany would have been close to his ideal of the "free" state. He did *not* glorify the Prussian State of his time. But he did not go far beyond it.

Hegel's political motivation is also apparent in the development of his more strictly philosophical positions, even in the

traditional disciplines of metaphysics and logic. He was aware
from the very beginning of the social relation between politics,
religion, morality, and ways of thinking. Thinking of course is
related to the activities of all disciplines but in the fields of
culture, if it goes wrong it directly affects our way of life. In his
Phenomenology of the Spirit, Hegel offers some graphic illustrations of the relation between ways of thought and ways of
cultural and political behavior. He is particularly critical of
"the understanding" of the French Enlightenment. Its logic
leads to a conception of freedom as something "simple, homo-
geneous, and uniform," as a force that "effaces and annuls all
social rank and classes which are the component spiritual
factors of the differentiated Whole." In the *Encyclopedia of the
Philosophical Sciences,* he is even more explicit. "The necessity
of understanding Logic in a wider sense than as the science of
the forms of thought is reinforced by the interests of religion
and politics, law and morality." Not the analytic *Verstand* but
the synthetic *Vernunft* is the appropriate instrument for
reaching concrete truth, especially in the realm of spirit or
"objective mind" which is close to the contemporary anthropol-
ogists' conception of Culture. The analytic understanding with
its appeal to abstractions and universals, out of time and the
historical process, has led to the Terror and the social convul-
sions of France. Since its ideals can never be realized, a
commitment to them functions like a built-in predisposition to
continuous revolution, purges and all. The logic of the analytic
understanding impelled Napoleon to impose "rational" Constitutions on nations historically unprepared for them. Not that
Hegel is opposed to Constitutions: he is opposed only to
drawing them up on the basis of first principles, rules of
reason, eternal rights. A Constitution must be "the work of
centuries," a slow growth in accordance with the genius of a
people and the "divine" Substance of history. The only good
revolutions are dead ones, like extinct volcanoes on whose
ridges of cooled lava a fertile soil can develop in time.

The logic of the *Begriff,* of the concrete universal, which is
central to Hegel's metaphysics and logic, is exquisitely adapted
to undercut the impatient claims of the understanding. It takes

over and reinterprets in a "higher" sense the principles of "freedom" and "reason" in whose name the radicals attempt to transform society. It substitutes reliance upon the gradual evolutionary processes of historical growth for the moralistic, revolutionary zeal which seeks to remake the world from scratch. The logic of the concrete universal is the logic of the system, not of the class or collection. It stresses interdependence of parts, differentiation, hierarchical organization. It allows for change: but an ordered and orderly change controlled by an immanent teleology whose ends are discerned by wise rulers advised by professional bureaucrats. It recognizes equality— not of sameness or of power or of function but of participation in social life, an equality of obligation to one's station and its duties. The concrete universal is a system which although out of time, embraces time. Therefore history properly understood is not a record merely of oppression, ignorance, and bloodshed— this results only when the understanding applies its axe of "reason" to social institutions—but of maturing wisdom. It recognizes human need but distinguishes it from desire; true utility but as something other than individual pleasure; experiment but only if we view history itself as the cummulative result of the experiments of the race and not as the contrived and planned experiment of the laboratory.

The organic system is the model of the concrete universal. The opposite of organic principles, like the abstractions the French used to reform political life, "spell in science as in politics, death to every rational concept, organization, and life."

Strictly speaking, the logic of the concrete universal does not entail the specific features of the corporate authoritarian society which Hegel counterposed both to the radical republicans, and the reactionary opponents of any social or political change, but it lends itself more easily to the purposes of those who wish to moderate rather than accelerate the pace of change. By professing to find both necessity and reason in history as given, it reinforces the natural prejudice in favor of the present order among its beneficiaries, and blunts the resentment of the discontented. It strengthens the *attitudes* of conservatism, of suspicion of plans of reform emanating from those not in authority, of horror of the thought (not to speak of the face) of revolution. This attitude finds expression on almost every relevant page of Hegel's writings. To be sure, he complains that he has been misunderstood by those who interpret him as identifying the "existent" with "the real" and "the rational." But he nowhere tells us when the "existent" becomes irrational. His judgment is always *ex post facto*. Like those who invoke God's Will and Wisdom in history, the exact equivalent of *die List der Vernunft,*[e] he is always wise *after* the event. Until then he is on the side of the "Powers that Be," or on the side of what is so powerfully in the making that the future is easy to read. This is the logic of unheroic conservatism whose first reaction to proposals for reform is "not yet" or "all in good time." Hegel's nationalism is the source of his failure to draw the obvious logical political corollary of the concrete universal, a world-state, and of his yearning for a leader who would use his own cunning to help out the Cunning of Reason in liberating Germany from the French invader and thus end national humiliation. Machiavellian villainy is eulogized in extravagant language when it serves the cause of national unity. Hegel's conservatism was a check on his nationalism. When nationalism became a popular mass movement, he feared it would get out of hand unless it was inoculated against the abstractions of the French political disease. Only a conservative and a nationalist like Bismarck could have fulfilled the role which Hegel outlined for the Machiavellian architect of the German Empire. It is not without significance that during the Bismarckian period, and indeed up to the first World War, when Hegel's panlogism was eclipsed because of the patent absurdities of his *Naturphilosophie* in an era of great scientific advance, he was universally regarded by the German Establishment as *"unser Nationalstaatsphilosoph."*[d]

---

[e] "The cunning of reason." W.K.

[d] I do not think that I have ever seen the phrase in quotes. The first part of this sentence seems to suggest that Hegel's panlogism was eclipsed only about the time of the First World War, but this claim is expressly disowned near the end of Professor Hook's final rejoinder. W.K.

This interpretation of Hegel is sharply opposed by Dr. Pelczynski and a number of other contemporary writers intent on claiming Hegel for the liberal tradition and reversing the judgment on him as a philosophical time-server of Metternichian reaction. According to Dr. Pelczynski, Hegel was a "champion of political rationality," in the same sense as Jeremy Bentham. The difference between them is to Hegel's credit, for whereas Bentham's moral utilitarianism prevented him from making sense of "natural rights" and "the law of reason," Hegel was their stout defender. "In this respect Hegel is much nearer Paine than Bentham." Not since the baptism of Aristotle has anything as bold as this transfiguration been attempted.

If Dr. Pelczynski's interpretation is valid, then we must indeed conclude that Hegel has been one of the most misunderstood of philosophers in the history of thought. But it seems to me, to put it mildly, to be invalid, as far from the truth about Hegel as the view which would make him a precursor or exponent of totalitarianism. Bentham was a political rationalist in the precise sense in which the thinkers of the Enlightenment were political rationalists whose abstractions about equality, freedom, and human happiness Hegel regarded as responsible for the social madness of the Terror and the despotism which followed the French Revolution. It is true that Bentham made sport of the rhetoric about natural rights; but what he failed to understand was that to Thomas Jefferson (and to Tom Paine) natural rights are reasonable rights. What was "reasonable" to them had nothing to do with the Hegelian *Vernunft* but was a common-sensical version of utilitarianism. The "reasonable" was what furthered human happiness or reduced unnecessary human suffering.

The most weighty evidence for Dr. Pelczynski's interpretation—aside from tortured exegesis of texts read in the light of an hypothesis assumed to be true—is Hegel's warm praise of the outbreak of the French Revolution. From the time he danced together with Schelling around a "Freedom Tree" (during his Tübingen period) to his death, Hegel kept green the memory of the French Revolution as a great event in the calendar of human freedom. He drank a toast to the Fall of the Bastille every July 14th. An entire brochure has been devoted to this and allied themes. Joachim Ritter in his *Hegel und die Revolution* runs through the references to the French Revolution in Hegel's works. He stresses all the words of praise, but unfortunately plays down or explains away all of Hegel's criticisms, reservations, and contemptuous references to those who opposed the Metternichian system.[e] For Ritter, Hegel's philosophy is an elaboration of the implications of the French principle of freedom for the *whole* of social life. How far he is prepared to go is apparent in the following passage anent the *Philosophy of Right:*

> The youthful enthusiasm for the Revolution which one finds at the outset of Hegel's philosophical career was absorbed into his philosophy and vitally expressed itself in its mature form. His philosophy remains in the precise sense the philosophy of revolution from which it took its point of departure and on which it flourishes to the end. There is nothing in Hegel's spiritual development that characterizes it better than this positive relation to Revolution: it determines both its end and beginning.

One is tempted to say that there is nothing more extravagant and false than this interpretation except possibly the view that Hegel was a Fascist. There are many passages in Hegel which run directly counter to this view. In the *Philosophy of Right,* which according to Ritter presupposes and elaborates the principle of freedom of the French Revolution, Hegel writes: [f]

---

[e] I am not sure to whom "those" refers. The four-volume *Hegel-Lexikon* to the twenty-volume *Jubiläumsausgabe* of Hegel's works, ed. H. Glockner, does not list a single reference to Metternich, nor does Hegel ever mention him in the four volumes of his published correspondence. w.k.

[f] To be precise, Hegel did not write the paragraph that follows; it is taken from the editor's "Addition" to § 5 in the posthumous edition. And in this case the Knox translation used by Hook is less than literal. What Hegel is here reported to have said in his lectures is this: " . . . This is where the period of the Terror during the French Revolution belongs, when the intention was to do away with all differences of talent, of authority. This time was a tremor, an earthquake, a refusal to tolerate anything individual; for fanaticism aims at something abstract, not a structure: where differences emerge, it finds that they are at odds with its own indeterminacy and it does away with them. Hence the people [*das Volk*] destroyed again during the Revolution the institutions that they themselves had created, because every institution is at odds with the abstract self-consciousness of equality." w.k.

This form of freedom appears more concretely in the active fanaticism of both political and religious life. For instance, during the Terror in the French Revolution all differences of talent and authority were supposed to have been superseded. This period was an upheaval, an agitation, an irreconcilable hatred of everything particular. Since fanaticism wills abstraction only, nothing articulated, it follows that when distinctions appear, it finds them antagonistic to its own indeterminacy and annuls them. For this reason the French Revolutionaries destroyed once more the institutions which they had made themselves, since any institution whatever is antagonistic to the abstract self-consciousness of equality.

But more than the citation, the matching and the explication of texts is involved. There is a certain naiveté in believing that to herald and praise the outbreak of the Revolution is to approve its course. The fall of the Bastille is an act which symbolizes the fall of the *ancien régime* not the rise of the new. In our own day how many are there who hailed the February and even the October Revolutions in Russia and still justify them (the first for the downfall of Czarism, the second for bringing World War I in the East to a close) who abominate its subsequent course? Even the Daughters of the American Revolution and the John Birch Society celebrate with great fervor on every July 4th, the events of 1776. Hegel at no time held a brief for the *ancien régime,* but from the moment it became apparent in any country that the stewards of social change were not to be bureaucrats and state officials but the tribunes of the people, ostensibly responsible to it and not to an autocrat or monarch, he became suspicious of its direction. He trembled even at the minor revolutionary waves of 1830. All of the writers who are seeking to recreate the image of Hegel are silent about the fact that he withdrew the preface of his *Philosophy of Right* from the printers in order to add a denunciation of the neo-Kantian philosopher, J. F. Fries, who, because of his participation in the Wartburg Festival, was in trouble with the police. Here as elsewhere the object of Hegel's attack was not the system of the Holy Alliance but those who were struggling against it. Herbert Marcuse contends that the *Burschenschaft* and others whom Hegel denounced were proto-Nazis; but this is absurd. If all who expressed anti-Semitic sentiments are to be considered Nazis, or "as bad as Nazis," we would have to include among the precursors of Hitler not only Voltaire but Marx himself. [g]

Perhaps those who see in Hegel a prophet of liberalism are using the term "liberalism" in a Pickwickian sense. It is wrong to assume with Russell that liberalism is necessarily wedded to empiricism or vice versa. Socially, the connections between the two are less than logical and more than merely psychological. A thinker can defend a liberal position on the basis of an idealistic (even theological) metaphysics in the sense that his justifying reasons are expressed in the idiom of his system or creed. But what defines a liberal position in social and political affairs? Not any one trait or program, to be sure, whether it is "free enterprise" or the conception of the state as a neutral umpire between warring social groups. There is a family of traits which define the liberal temper, several of which must be present before we can justifiably classify a thinker as *liberal.* Among the things we look for in a liberal thinker are recognition of the moral primacy of the individual in appraising institutional life, acceptance of a free market of *ideas,* tolerance of political opposition, appreciation of diversity, openmindedness to alternatives, endorsement of the right to self-determination, national, social and personal, including the moral right to revolution if the demand for self-determination is persistently frustrated. And, underlying all, reliance on the methods of intelligence conceived not as Reason carrying out ends of which we are not aware, but as common sense fortified by relevant scientific knowledge. Liberalism is not so much a doctrine as an attitude toward political affairs which is aware of human finitude and the tentativeness of human judgment and yet is prepared to act vigorously in moments of crisis. When it is given to religious language, it regards the ascription of Perfection or Divinity to the State (which we find in Hegel), or to any other human institution, as blasphemous.

[g] For Fries, see section 5 of the final essay, below; for the relevant quotation from Marcuse, section 12. W.K.

One need read only a few pages of any of Hegel's works that touch on culture and history to sense how far he is from the liberal outlook. In feeling and judgment, he is a natural conservative. His system of ideas gives him a bias in favor of the established. His temperament perhaps, rather than his general position, accounts for the fact that in moments of crisis he was more likely to be a fellow-traveller of the reactionaries (although critical of their faults) than a friend of social reformers (except when the reforms come from those already in power). But his general position made it easier for him to rationalise his timidities and fears.

Nonetheless there is something that contemporary liberals can learn from Hegel. This is the importance of the principles of continuity and polarity in avoiding lapses into doctrinaire positions. History abounds with illustrations, and we need not go far in our own time to find them. Not every plausible plan is a workable one. Readiness is not all—the ripeness and maturity of conditions, independently determined, count for something too. We cannot wipe out history and begin as if we were born yesterday. There is no one principle that can guide us in human affairs whether it be the principle of freedom, peace, survival, justice, love, or what not. Each one exacts a price in terms of the others. Effective as these and similar maxims are in diminishing the risks of excess, by themselves they do not constitute an adequate philosophy. All they add up to is a counsel of caution.

Despite contentions to the contrary, the philosophy of the Enlightenment in its best exemplars, save for its optimism and absence of the tragic sense of life, took note of the dangers Hegel feared. Except for Rousseau, whose false and mischievous doctrine of the "general will" Hegel took over, they were free from obscurantic romanticism. For all his invocations to Reason, Hegel distrusted the critical and sceptical spirit of the Enlightenment, its striving for clarity, its exposure of theological and philosophical humbug. The Hegelian philosophy did not become, except for its fetishism of the State, the ideology of the counterrevolutionary restoration. Hegel's ambiguities had somewhat the same disturbing effect upon conservative circles as Hobbes' doctrines upon the Royalists of his day. Nonetheless its intent was to undermine the mode of thinking which inspired the French Revolution.

6 *Hook's Hegel*

SHLOMO AVINERI

Professor Sidney Hook's essay on the Knox-Pelczynski edition of *Hegel's Political Writings* pinpoints most of the issues crucial to any discussion of Hegel's political thinking. It is not, however, free from some of the misconceptions which have bedeviled this discussion in the past two generations.

While rejecting Karl Popper's diatribe against Hegel, Professor Hook maintains that Hegel was a "German nationalist from the very *beginning* of his career" and that during the Bismarckian period "he was universally regarded by the German Establishment as *unser Nationalphilosoph.*" Both statements, I am afraid, fly in the face of textual and historical evidence.

If Hegel were a nationalist "from the very *beginning* of his career," this would have to be proved from his *Early Theologi-*

71

cal Writings, which predate *The German Constitution* by several years. Yet an examination of these essays reveals that the only passages which have any bearing on problems of nationalism are *vehemently anti-nationalist* and totally opposed to the romantic notions of the German nationalist literature of that period. Hegel dismisses the Herderian tradition of reviving the German *Ur-Mythos* and *Ur-Volk,* maintaining that the old Germanic tradition

> has nothing in our day to connect or adapt itself to; it stands as cut off from the whole circle of our ideas, opinions and beliefs, and it is as strange as the imagery of Ossian or of India (*Hegel's Early Theological Writings,* Knox-Kroner edition, p. 149).

As for the essay on *The German Constitution,* one usually tends to forget the perhaps trivial yet not totally insignificant fact that the original manuscript had no title, and that the now famous title *Die Verfassung Deutschlands* dates from Georg Mollat's first full edition of this essay in 1893. More than a mere title is involved here. A careful study of this long essay suggests that the question of German unification on a national-ist basis hardly figures in the manuscript, and that what Hegel is really after is the reform of the structure and institutional traditions of the German politico-social system. What Hegel critizes is the *absence of any sort of political authority in Germany.* When he starts his essay with the bombshell "*Deutschland ist kein Staat mehr,*"[a] he does not have *national* uni-fication in mind, but the creation of some kind, of any kind, of authority which would be *political* in the Hegelian sense— *i.e.,* universalistic and not particularistic, an authority which could safeguard the common, and not private, interests. Hegel criticizes the existing hotch-potch of kingdoms, principalities, bishoprics, duchies, landgravates and free imperial cities not as an impediment to national unity, which does not concern him at all, but as a stumbling block to the emergence of modern political life in Germany. He does not even accord the German

---

[a] "Germany is no longer a state." W.K.

petty states the honor of referring to them as "states." Throughout the essay he contemptuously dismisses them as mere "estates" (*Stände*), belonging rather to the egotistic and particularistic civil society than to the universal realm of the state. Their very existence makes political life in Germany impossible.

Far from dealing with the quest for national unity, the whole essay is concerned with proposals for the reform of the anti-quated, medieval, stagnant socio-political fabric of Germany, and this is brought out most clearly by Dr. Pelczynski in his Introductory Essay. Moreover, Hegel feels that the nonexis-tence of a political organization in Germany is the cause of a dangerous political vacuum in Central Europe. Believing in the idea of a European Balance of Power (surely a prenationalist notion), Hegel feels that the existence of some sort of political organization in Germany is required and that this could be achieved only by doing away with Germany's hybrid combina-tion of feudalism and petty-absolutism. A German "1789" was needed, and the essay is really the adaptation of the ideas of the French Revolution to German reality. In this essay Hegel emerges as the most radical opponent of the German *status quo*. Whatever his later conservative sins might have been, there is nothing of subservience, timidity, or time-serving here.

Significantly, Hegel does not even consider the original Prus-sian territory to be part of the reconstituted political entity of Germany. The Prussian state itself is for Hegel a lifeless, sterile mechanism (*Hegel's Political Writings*, pp. 163–164); it is spiritless, narrowly bureaucratic, and mechanistic. Freedom, which for Hegel consists of representation and modern political institutions, can be safeguarded only by a state "which itself rests on this system of freedom." Since "without a representa-tive body, freedom is no longer thinkable" (p. 234), Prussia is naturally ruled out as the lever for political modernization in Germany. Few German writers have criticised Frederician Prussia in harsher terms.

Furthermore, Hegel considers national or ethnic characteris-tics irrelevant to the modern state, and I find it really difficult to understand how Professor Hook can conceive as "a nationalist" a writer who had the following to say about ethnico-national ties:

> In our day the tie between members of a state in respect of manners, education, language may be rather loose or even non-existent. Identity in these matters, once the foundation of a people's union, is now to be reckoned amongst the accidents whose character does not hinder a mass from constituting a public authority. . . . Thus dissimilarity in culture and manners is a necessary product as well as a necessary condition of the stability of the modern states.

In an earlier draft of *The German Constitution* which is not included in the Knox-Pelczynski edition, Hegel cites some examples:

> The powerful Austrian and Russian monarchs rule over many languages which do not even have a common origin. . . . The languages of many provinces of France and England differ from the dominant language. . . . In Wales and the Hebrides English is not spoken at all. . . .

With such ideas in his mind, there is no wonder that Hegel's political allegiance during the Napoleonic Wars was anything but that of a German nationalist. 1813 is the true shibboleth of early nineteenth-century German nationalism, and Professor Hook completely overlooks Hegel's attitude during that early period.

In 1806, Hegel most explicitly welcomed the Prussian defeat at Jena, writing to a friend that he "wishes the French victory and success" and calling Napoleon a "World Soul" (*Weltseele*) and "the Great Constitutional Lawyer of Paris." This follows most clearly from the ideas expounded in the so-called *The German Constitution.* Napoleon put a drastic end to the medieval anarchy in Germany, introduced rational legislation, and a codification based on universal norms and principles rather than on positive, historical law. After all, Napoleon's transformation of Germany corresponded for the most part to

Hegel's own blueprint of political reform in *The German Constitution*. It was no idle conjecture on the part of some of Hegel's commentators to suggest that Hegel actually had Napoleon in mind when he spoke in 1802 of "a German Theseus." Hence Hegel's hostile attitude to the German anti-French insurrection in 1813, hence his support for Napoleon up to the bitter end and his final moving lament after Waterloo: "Our great Napoleon—who would have ever thought this would, could, have been his end" (Hegel's *Briefe*, II, p. 23).

Far from being a servile supporter of Metternichian reaction, Hegel is full of criticism of the Vienna Congress and the reactionary measures enacted by it: this can be easily seen from his correspondence in 1815–1820 with Niethammer, Fromann, Hinrichs, von Tadden, *et al.* The only satisfaction the Vienna arrangements brought him was the fact that no central authority was established in Germany and that the clamor for German unity did not prevail in the Councils of Europe. "The nonsensical arrangement called the German Empire . . . reached the end it deserved" is his final verdict in 1816.

But then why was Hegel in favor of a central political authority in Germany in 1802 and opposed to it in 1816? The answer to this lies in the fact that the historical situation had changed completely. Not only had the number of political units in Germany been reduced from some 300 to 37, but most of them had been completely overhauled, modernized, and developed from patrimonial "estates" into modern political states. Varying degrees of representative institutions had been introduced; a codified rational law replaced the archaic monstrosities of case law; a relatively enlightened bureaucracy based on the Napoleonic principle of *carrière ouverte aux talents* ruled where earlier nepotism, corruption, incompetence had held sway. This was achieved either directly by French administration or pressure (as in Rhineland-Westphalia, Bavaria, Württemberg) or by way of response to the French challenge (as in Prussia). These modern states did not need any superimposed political machinery which the medieval "estates" of 1802 needed so badly; they were themselves modern states.

When Hegel opposed the nationalist movement after 1815 it was precisely because the nationalists wanted to replace these modern, rationally-organized states by what amounts to a romantic chimera of a subjective idea of an idealized German medieval past. They wanted to do away with modern, rational codification and replace it by traditional German law. They were historicist, traditionalist, anti-rationalist, anti-French and anti-Enlightenment (hence also their anti-Semitism). When Hegel attacked one of the nationalist leaders, Fries, it was not because he was a Kantian (of sorts), nor because "Fries was in trouble with the police," as suggested by Professor Hook. It was because Fries' Wartburg Address was one of the worst demagogic, fanatical, obscurantist, and racialist outbursts of German chauvinism. It is surely ironical that this dark corner of German history should find in Professor Hook one of its defenders.

Sidney Hook takes it for granted that Hegel was considered by the Bismarckian Establishment as a German nationalist philosopher. The facts, however, seem to indicate something quite different. *Prior to 1870, nobody ever identified Hegel with German nationalism.* On the contrary, the most influential image of Hegel in Germany was the one represented in Rudolf Haym's *Hegel und seine Zeit* (published in 1857), where Hegel is impeached as a traitor to German nationalism and unification. Nobody ever seriously questioned this till 1870, especially as Hegel's connection with Prussia meant that he was allied to the most anti-nationalist power in early nineteenth-century Germany.

By referring to Hegel as *"unser Nationalphilosoph,"* Professor Hook is probably alluding to Karl Rosencranz's book *Hegel als deutscher Nationalphilosoph.* It must be noted that the year of its publication (1870) was not only the centenary of Hegel's birth; it was also the high tide of German nationalism, and Rosencranz's book is a most tedious and deplorable study in nationalistic apologetics. It is vastly inferior to his two earlier books on Hegel, where very little is said about nationalism. When he wrote this third book about his master in 1870, he was an old and ailing man, setting out (as he admits in his Introduction) to save Hegel from the political wilderness into which he had been driven by the *Sturm und Drang* of German nationalism. Not only is it a rambling, gossipy work of a failing intellect: one has to read it to realize how misleading its title is even on Rosencranz's own premises. Rosencranz himself does not claim that Hegel was a nationalist in his political outlook. What he really sets out to do is to vindicate Hegel as a German literary classic, much like Goethe. This may or may not be true, but it has little to do with Hegel's political attitudes; nor did the general textbooks of philosophy or history in the Bismarckian period have anything else to say about Hegel in regard to his nationalism.

For Hegel was always considered as a sort of dangerous alien by the full-blooded German nationalists. Not only the Nazis thought his philosophy smacked of something Jewish (if one may borrow Professor Hook's expression). As early as the 1830s, an anonymous writer (probably O. H. Gruppe) produced an amusing if otherwise worthless verse comedy which lampooned Hegel as *"Absolutus, Philosoph zu Utopien,"* surrounded by a garlic-smelling coterie of students—Arroganz, Absalom, and Israel, the sons of Aaron Gans, "A Jewish Innkeeper and Distiller of Concrete Spirit." On a more serious level, K. E. Schubart attacked Hegel's philosophy as totally alien to the Prussian tradition and suggested that it be banned from the universities, as it is "totally inimical to the Prussian state, constitutes a threat to undermine the existing order of the body politic and to bring about sedition and rebellion. . . ."

This brings one to the question of Hegel's attitude to Prussia. Prussia is a dirty word nowadays, and much misunderstanding has been caused by a semantic projection of the image of post-1870 Prussia on to the earlier periods. But the nineteenth century knew at least four "Prussias." There was the military Hohenzollern-cum-Junker state, "an army in possession of a state," which received its death blow at Jena in 1806. There was the reformed, enlightened Prussia of von Stein and Hardenberg. Then the romantic, pietistic, pseudo-medieval

Prussia of Friedrich Wilhelm IV. And finally, the nationalist Prussia of Bismarck. Hegel detested the first Prussia, as is made clear in *The German Constitution* and in his remarks about the Prussian defeat at Jena. He was virtually ostracized by the third—Friedrich Wilhelm IV summoned the aging Schelling to Berlin University to stamp out the Hegelian heritage root and branch. It is hardly imaginable that Hegel would have welcomed Bismarck's Prusso-Germany, which was the worst combination of Prussian *Junkertum,* pietistic humbug, and romantic nationalism. It was the second Prussia, Prussia of the Age of Reform, with which Hegel identified himself. Surely Professor Hook would agree that given the German circumstances of 1815–1830, this certainly was not the worst of choices. Or is anyone who wasn't a Jacobin at that time anathema?[1]

The point, however, is that Hegel backed the wrong horse. Though anticipating many of the traits of the modern state, Hegel was basically rather out of touch with his own *Zeitgeist.* His idealized version of a reformed, effectively run Prussia, headed by an enlightened monarch and a "universal class" of bureaucrats (in a way, a Napoleonic empire without Napoleonic *grandeur*) never materialized. Hegel idealized it even while it was already breaking up.[2]

Romanticism and nationalism, both of which he detested, got the upper hand, and Hegel's political philosophy remained one of the Lost Causes of German history, along with the noble aspirations of von Stein—and Goethe. Fichte's disciples, with their subjectivist ethics, nationalistic *mores,* and totalitarian tendencies (*cf.* Fichte's *The Closed Commercial State*) obliterated the delicate autonomy of Hegel's Civil Society and subordinated it to the nationalist dream that was to turn European history into a nightmare. How far Hegel himself became one of the major victims of his own inability to read his own *Zeitgeist* correctly is evident from the fact that he is even held responsible for the movement which turned him into one of its first victims. A very sad commentary indeed on *die List der Vernunft.*

NOTES

1. Some recent re-appraisals of Hegel's political philosophy include: Walter Kaufmann, "The Hegel Myth," in his *From Shakespeare to Existentialism* (1960) [included in the present volume] and his just-published *Hegel: Reinterpretation, Texts and Commentary* (Doubleday, 1965); Leon J. Goldstein, "The Meaning of 'State' in Hegel's Philosophy of History," *The Philosophical Quarterly* (January 1962); and Eugène Fleischmann, *La philosophie politique de Hegel* (Paris, 1964).
2. On this see my "Hegel and Nationalism," *Review of Politics* (October 1962) [included in the present volume]; also "Hegel and War," *Journal of the History of Ideas* (October-December 1961).

7 *Hegel Again*

Z. A. PELCZYNSKI

I am grateful to Sidney Hook for focusing his review article so sharply and accurately on the problem of Hegel's basic political attitude, which is indeed the central theme of my introduction to *Hegel's Political Writings*. I am very glad to have his support for my conviction, which was the *raison d'être* of my essay, that the political writings do throw important light on that complex and controversial problem. But I failed to grasp how after reading the political writings he can maintain his own interpretation of Hegel and dismiss so absolutely the one I have put forward. Although he professes to steer a middle course between those who, like Karl Popper, have painted Hegel in the darkest colors as a proto-Nazi and an enemy of an "open society," and those like Joachim Ritter, John Plamenatz and myself who, allegedly, seek to pass off Hegel, scrubbed and whitewashed, as "a prophet of liberalism," it is difficult to see where Professor Hook's moderation really lies. There is a difference of degree in the unobjectivity of his and Popper's approach, but basically "Hegel Rehabilitated?" is yet another political tract, an outburst of righteous liberal-democratic-radical indignation, all the more powerful and persuasive since the underlying political passion is kept under control and released in carefully graduated doses.

By imputing political passion to Professor Hook I am deliberately choosing a charitable explanation of the one-sided and tendentious account which he gives of Hegel's political attitude in his article. If I am guilty, in my interpretation of Hegel's writings, of "tortured exegesis of texts read in the light of a hypothesis assumed to be true," I hope I cannot be accused of having simplified my task by passing over substantial portions of the texts which contradicted the hypothesis. But this is just what Professor Hook has done again and again. One striking example of this technique: to show that Hegel disparaged liberty as liberal-democrats understand it, Professor Hook quotes the beginning of a paragraph in *The German Constitution,* where Hegel speaks contemptuously of a "blind clamour of freedom." Let me continue the quotation beyond the place where Professor Hook interrupts it. After the words "trying to embrace the cloud [of freedom], the nations have flung themselves into an abyss of misery . . .," Hegel goes on to say,

. . . and definite concepts and forms of thought have become embodied in public opinion. Clamour for freedom will have no effect; anarchy has become distinguished from freedom; the notion that a firm government is indispensable for freedom has become deeply engraved on men's minds; *but no less deeply engraved is the notion that the people must share in the making of laws and the management of the most important affairs of state. The guarantee that the government will proceed in accordance with law, and the co-operation of the general will in the most important affairs of state which affect everyone, the people finds in the organisation of a body representative of the people.* This body has to sanction payment to the monarch of part of the national taxes, but especially the payment of extraordinary taxes. Just as in former days the most important matter, *i.e.,* personal services, depended on free agreement, so nowadays money, which comprises influence of every other kind, is equally so dependent.

Without such a representative body, freedom is no longer thinkable. Once freedom is so defined, all vague ideas vanish, along with all the emptiness of the clamour for freedom. This notion of freedom is not something, like a scientific concept, which individuals come to know by learning; on the contrary, it is a fundamental principle in public opinion; it has become part of sound common sense. . . . (*Hegel's Political Writings,* pp. 234, 235. My italics.)

Is this the language of an authoritarian thinker, a supporter of absolutism and fellow-traveller of reaction, to mention some of the terms Professor Hook applies to Hegel? By leaving out the rest of the passage just quoted, does he not give a wholly false impression of Hegel's concept of political freedom?

Hegel's concept of representation is certainly not "progressive" by mid-twentieth or even mid-nineteenth-century standards. But is it possible to deny, on the evidence of the *Political Writings,* that he belonged to a constitutionalist or whig-liberal current of political thought, traceable to Kant, Montesquieu, Locke, and beyond, which is the source of modern liberalism? If his life-span (1770–1831) and the age-long dominance of absolutism in his native Germany are remembered, Hegel's hesitation to allow the popular masses a more influential role in government becomes perfectly intelligible. Nor does the fear of "mob rule" necessarily exclude Hegel from the liberal tradition. Unimpeachably liberal thinkers from Tocqueville and J. S. Mill to Ortega y Gasset and Walter Lippmann have been as sensitive to its dangers as he was.

Equally one-sided is Professor Hook's other view, viz., that Hegel rejected absolute human rights, and paid scant attention to the interests and welfare of individuals. But Hegel regarded the guaranteeing of such rights and constitutional protection of individual interests as a mark of a rational constitution which, incidentally, contrary to what Professor Hook alleges, had according to Hegel to be formulated on the basis of universal principles. In the essay on the *Würtemberg Estates* Hegel takes for granted the rights such as "Every subject is at liberty to choose his profession and occupation according to his free inclination, and to educate himself for it" are "organic provisions which speak for themselves and make up the rational basis of constitutionalism." They must be in the constitution as "a matter of principle, i.e., of rationality and absolute right." "They do the greatest honour to the prince who gave them and to the age in which constitutional law has been purged of privileges and matured into a [set] of principles." They are "universal truths of constitutionalism," and so on. Hegel never disparaged "the famous *Droits de l'homme et du citoyen*"; he only insisted that they could not be operative until they were particularized in legislation and administrative procedures. Hegel's "civil society" is precisely the sphere of the modern state where authorities of various kinds subserve individual rights, interests, and happiness. Only exigencies of public peace or national survival justify the invasion of that sphere by the "political state" as the guardian of the people's common interest.

By calling Hegel a "nationalist" throughout his article Professor Hook reaches the summit of misrepresentation. Perhaps the most serious criticism that can be made of Hegel's concept of the modern state is precisely that he ignored the force of nationalism in the modern world. Probably for that very reason he considered hereditary monarchy a necessary focus of loyalty and an element of solidarity within the state. It is true that in *The German Constitution* Hegel resented the humiliation of Germany by France and was preoccupied with German unity,[1] but shortly afterward Hegel abandoned all thought of German unification and in 1818 openly welcomed the creation of a sovereign Würtemberg state as "one of the actual German realms which are taking the place of the nonentity which had borne only the empty name of an 'Empire.'..." In the preface to the *Philosophy of Right,* Hegel showed unmistakable hostility to the idea of immediate German unity. One can, in his later life, accuse him of Prussian patriotism but never of German nationalism. His position was that any state was worthy of loyalty and obedience as long as it was rationally organized, whether its population formed one nation, a section of a nation, or a group of nations.

Equally incorrect, I suggest, is Professor Hook's interpretation of Hegel's attitude to the French Revolution. There is much that Hegel disliked about the Revolution or, more strictly, the period of revolutionary changes between 1789 and 1815 which have frequently been lumped together. But it is undeniable that he regarded the Revolution (in this wider sense) as the most significant event in modern history since the Reformation. The evidence for it is not in anecdotes about dancing round a freedom tree or drinking toasts on Bastille Day, but in Hegel's public pronouncements. In the essay on *Würtemberg Estates* (published when Hegel was forty-eight and a professor at Heidelberg) he calls the years since 1789 "possibly the richest that the world history has had and for us the most instructive because our world and our ideas belong to them." And in his lectures on *The Philosophy of History,* last delivered at Berlin University shortly before his death, Hegel interpreted the Revolution as the culmination of the process of liberating mankind from the shackles of tradition, prejudice, and dogma which began in the Reformation, and the beginning of the re-shaping of social and political reality by rational thought, "a glorious mental dawn." How can Professor Hook label Hegel an opponent of the Revolution and a conservative when Hegel almost foamed at the mouth at the mention of "antiquity," "wisdom of forefathers," "veneration of the past," and consistently championed the fundamental principle of the Revolution that in the social and political sphere "nothing should be recognised as valid unless its recognition accorded with the right of reason."[2]

The argument that Hegel turned the significance of the Revolution upside down by giving "reason" and "rational" a special sinister meaning is rather weak. Whatever the metaphysical nuances and implications of these terms, on the practical and political level which is at issue between Professor Hook and myself, Hegel's "reason" and "rational" incorporate most of all, the substance of what revolutionary thinkers meant by these terms. Hegel did not reject their ideas *in toto*; he merely argued that in the name of logic they pressed "freedom," "equality," "popular sovereignty," etc., to extreme and therefore untenable conclusions and paid inadequate attention to the social and political costs of their schemes. He was profoundly sceptical of impatient perfectionism, and saw that no state could subsist without reconciling immaculate revolutionary ideals and other principles, i.e., authority, solidarity, hierarchy, and so on. As Hegel said in *The German Constitution*, freedom without order was anarchy, just as strong government without people's participation was tyranny.

Professor Hook dubbed this aspect of Hegel's attitude "unheroic conservatism," but this label, like his whole approach, is fundamentally unfair. There is nothing unheroic about the determination, so clearly stated (*e.g.*, at the beginning of *The English Reform Bill* or in the preface to the *Philosophy of Right*) to criticize shallow ideas even when they are fashionable or can command a large popular following. There is nothing unheroic in telling social and political thinkers *hic Rhodus, hic saltus*: stop dreaming about utopias and give us theories by which we can understand reality and shape it in the light of our ideals. There is nothing unheroic about the attempt (however premature) to discover, beneath the flux of events, the shape of the emerging modern state. Not "unheroic conservatism" but "heroic realism" is the *mot juste* for Hegel's basic attitude.

Long before the time of Hegel or Thomas Paine there had been a tradition of constitutional government, rule of law, and civil rights. Generations of thinkers who had died long before them had rejected the claims of *mere* tradition and ancient institutions, and advocated a rational approach to political problems. In that sense, neither Hegel nor Paine were prophets of liberalism, but the one and the other shared its fundamental assumptions. They belonged, if I may so put it, to the right and the left of liberalism. One's preference for one or the other is largely a matter of taste and temperament. Few would deny, however, that the modern liberal democratic state is characterized by strong central government, a powerful executive, a large bureaucratic and military apparatus, an establishment of professional politicians, the organization of the electorate into mass political parties and a complex network of organized interest groups. This inescapable reality bears far closer resemblance to Hegel's concept of the modern state than do the pipedreams of early republicans, democrats, and radicals. My reply to Professor Hook's raised eyebrows about "Hegel Rehabilitated?" is—yes.

NOTES

1. Even that work is largely free from the nationalist myths ("organic unity," "intrinsic superiority," "civilizing mission") which later Fichte and others were to popularize in Germany.
2. It can be granted that Hegel was not "progressive" in the sense of going beyond the Revolution in propounding new principles. He merely demanded the realization of principles already asserted in the French Revolution. Yet the political rights which he advocated were still largely denied in central, eastern, and southern Europe, and even in western Europe many civil rights were still withheld (e.g., Jews, Dissenters, and Catholics in Britain).

8 *Hegel and His Apologists*

SIDNEY HOOK

In reading the passionate replies of Drs. Avineri and Pelczynski to my review-article of *Hegel's Political Writings,* I had somewhat the same feeling—making allowance for the difference in subject-matter—one normally experiences in reading a disquisition by circle-squarers. After all, I made no startling claim in maintaining that Hegel was a conservative, national thinker, *not* a racist, *not* a totalitarian. What I was mostly concerned to show was that to the extent extra-philosophical motives influenced Hegel's thought, and there is considerably more to his thought than his political philosophy, his early commitments throw light on the origin and development of his doctrine of the concrete universal and some of the inconsistencies of its application. To be charged with perverse misrepresentation of Hegel when I could more plausibly be taxed with accepting the conventional designation of him seems to me to be positively bizarre. Most expositors of Hegel, and not only his critics, have regarded Hegel as a conservative thinker as far as his own doctrines and allegiance go. They may all be wrong. Nonetheless until that is clearly established, it is somewhat startling to read that Hegel was not a conservative but a liberal, and indeed, a liberal like Tom Paine! And almost as startling is to read the heated denial that Hegel was a nationalist.

In my rejoinder I shall try to show that Hegel cannot legitimately be regarded as a liberal in either thought or practice, that his social and political philosophy is closer to Edmund Burke than to Tom Paine, and that he was a German nationalist in the sense I ascribed to him. To say this is not to say that Hegel's position is identical with Burke's or that his nationalism is like that of Father Jahn or of any other romantic fanatic.

I shall begin by citing a few pieces of "external" evidence to show how extraordinary is the judgment that Hegel was a liberal, "external" in that no exegesis of Hegel's text is required to understand them.

1. Hegel opposed the French Revolution of 1830 and even more bitterly the English Reform Bill of 1831. His grounds of opposition are instructive. He did not deny the existence of abuses and injustices in the prevailing system of representation and in society at large. But he feared far more the broadening of the electoral base. For this might well lead to social and political revolution. Hegel agrees with the fears expressed by the Duke of Wellington that if the Bill is adopted "in the place of those to whom the care of the public is now entrusted in Parliament, altogether different men will arrive. . . ." And like Wellington, Hegel denies that "shopkeepers of whom the great majority of voters will consist as a result of the new bill" are fit to elect those who must make decisions on domestic and foreign affairs. The whole essay (and not this essay alone) expresses a contempt for popular rule and a preference for a self-perpetuating bureaucracy of officials inspired by Reason. To be sure, one can be a liberal and distrustful of the sovereignty of the people and hedge it about with certain restraints, but in the last analysis liberalism accepts the view that government must be responsible to the people. For Hegel, however, government owes responsibility only to the State as Reason—the metaphysical abstraction which concealed the realities of power in absolutist Germany, and anywhere else it has been invoked. The flavor of Hegel's "liberalism" may be gathered from the invidious comparisons he draws between France and England, on the one hand, and Germany on the other. He refers to the principles behind the rights and laws "as reconstituted in the civilized States of the Continent . . . principles which, being grounded on universal Reason, cannot always remain so foreign even to the English understanding, as they have been hitherto." He then goes on to say that the *novi homines,* whom the Duke of Wellington rightly fears, will make use of these principles in "opposition to the government and the existing order of things; and the principles themselves would have to appear not in their practical truth and application, as in Germany (*sic!*) but in the dangerous form of French abstraction." It was, I have argued, to combat the appeal of "French abstractions," which tested principles by their empirical consequences in the everyday life of the people, that Hegel elaborated his organic logic.

2. Compare Hegel's position with the views expressed by Paine on the nature of the state and government. To Paine they are at best necessary evils: to Hegel, divinely blessed and the condition of all virtue. When the liberal descendants of Paine learn that state and government must have positive and not merely restraining functions this is interpreted in a purely instrumental and utilitarian sense utterly foreign to Hegel's fetishism of the state as a "supreme and absolute end-in-itself."

But the starkest contrast is to be found in their attitudes toward monarchy. Paine regarded the English Constitution as compounded of two tyrannies and one principle of republicanism. The tyrannies are monarchical and aristocratic; the republican element is embodied in the Commons "on whose virtue depends the freedom of England" (*Common Sense*). Hegel would have strengthened Paine's two principles of tyranny with the sole provision that they be exercised with Reason (which is decidedly *not* common sense). For Paine, monarchy is an evil and hereditary succession, a folly. He observes sardonically "nature disapproves hereditary right in kings, otherwise she would not so frequently turn it into ridicule, by giving mankind *an ass for a lion.*"

Now turn to Hegel's *Rechtsphilosophie* (Sec. 275 ff.) in which by the most specious reasoning that ever disgraced a philosopher, he tries to "prove" by Hegelian logic that state sovereignty must be embodied not merely in an individual, not merely in a monarch, but in a hereditary monarch! No wonder Hegel declares that this feat is beyond the power of "the understanding" (281). "The majesty of the monarch is a topic for thoughtful treatment by philosophy alone, since every method of inquiry, other than speculative method of the infinite Ideas which is purely self-grounded (Reason), annuls the nature of majesty altogether." It is difficult to tell what is more nauseating in writing of this kind—its sycophancy or its obfuscation. Were it not for their impassioned earnestness about Hegel's liberalism and basic affinity to Paine, I would suspect my critics of a sly joke.

3. Hegel explicitly critizes the philosophy of liberalism, identifying it not only by doctrine but by name. The trouble with liberalism, as Hegel sees it, is that it is too empirical; it wants individuals to rule as well as to be ruled. Not satisfied with the corporately organized state in which all citizens have reasonably determined functions, rights, and duties, under the influence and leadership of the intelligent members of the community, "*Liberalism* sets up in opposition to all this the atomistic principle, that which insists upon the sway of individual wills; maintaining that all government should emanate from their express power and have their express sanction." (*Philosophy of History.*) One may choose to defend Hegel's "enlightened" bureaucratic absolutism out of fear of "the dictatorship of the majority" but it is a crude terminological impropriety to call it "liberalism." From the time of Paine and Jefferson to the present, liberals, although aware of the dangers of popular

government, have had greater faith in the judgment of the citizenry *where a free market in ideas obtains,* than in the dictatorship of *any* minority.

4. A sharp light on Hegel's "liberalism" is thrown by his attitudes toward, and behavior in, Prussia. "Prussia is a dirty word nowadays," complains Dr. Avineri in his attempted whitewash of Hegel's role as a philosophical watchdog of the Prussian régime. It was what happened in Prussia in Hegel's time that made Prussia a by-word in the liberal circles of the day. It was Hegels ignoble behavior in contrast with thinkers like Schleiermacher, Humboldt, de Wette, and others that left an ineradicable stain on his name.

Hegel accepted the call to the University of Berlin *after* the Prussian restoration had begun—*after* the Wartburg Festival when the persecutions of those who called for a unified and constitutional Germany were at their height—and after the infamous rescript of Frederick William III of 21 March 1818, in which in crude and arrogant language the people were told that only the King in his own good time would redeem his promise to grant a constitution, and sternly warned that even a *petition* for a constitution "would awaken my well-founded displeasure." The repressive Carlsbad Decrees were in the offing. They were promulgated before Hegel sent his *Rechtsphilosophie* to the press and supported by him. As von Stein's letters make clear, Dr. Avineri to the contrary notwithstanding, this was *not* "the reformed, enlightened Prussia" for which the liberals had striven.

Absolutist governments have a keen eye for the uses of ideology. When such a régime gives official approval and support to a philosophical doctrine, this is far more weighty evidence of its social significance than the intentions of its propounder or the excuses of apologists. In the secret state archives of Prussia, Heinrich von Treitschke found a letter from Altenstein (the Prussian Minister of Education) to the King of Prussia, written after Hegel's death, in which he wrote: "In the Prussian State a solidly founded philosophical system has now put an end to arrogant and deplorable doings. The ministry cannot extend its aegis over any other philosophy and least of all over that of Schelling" (*History of Germany in the 19th Century*). This reference to Schelling, who was then passed over for an Hegelian nobody, is doubly significant. For in the early forties, when the Hegelian philosophy had been discredited at Court because of the young-Hegelian revolt and Schelling began to develop the reactionary views of his *Offenbarungsphilosophie*, he was called to Berlin and new appointments denied to Hegelians in any field except aesthetics.

We did not have to wait, however, for relevations from secret archives to know what the Prussian government thought of Hegel. Rosenkranz, Hegel's biographer, published a letter from Altenstein to Hegel (24 August 1821) after the appearance of the *Rechtsphilosophie* in which Hegel is warmly praised for conceiving the function of philosophy to be the discovery of Reason in nature, history, and the present, and thus preventing the public from applying "arbitrary ideals to the State." Dr. Avineri is undoubtedly aware of the letter since Haym also refers to it (*Hegel und seine Zeit,* p. 367) as the one in which Hegel is officially proclaimed "the Prussian Restoration State Philosopher."

Instead of addressing himself to evidence of this character, Dr. Avineri quotes some reactionary, if not crackpot, denunciations of Hegel to suggest that Hegel's philosophy is "totally alien to the Prussian tradition" and "totally inimical to the Prussian State." I find this procedure intellectually scandalous. Unless Dr. Avineri has evidence to the contrary, we have every reason to assume that Altenstein and the Prussian police bureaucracy were more qualified judges of what was inimical to the Prussian state than hysterical political and religious fundamentalists. The fact that a conservative is attacked by reactionaries does not transform him into a liberal! I wonder whether, e.g., Eisenhower, who is a simple-minded conservative, will be hailed as a liberal by some future Dr. Avineri because he has been denounced by the head of the John Birch Society as a Communist!

5. Not only did Hegel's thought become the house philosophy of the Prussian régime, Hegel's behavior toward the liberals of his day (and especially J. F. Fries) represented a betrayal of liberal principles. As Rosenkranz himself dolefully admits, Hegel's preface to his *Rechtsphilosophie* was considered an abomination in liberal circles during the whole of Hegel's subsequent lifetime. Hegel had recalled his proofs from the printer in order to add a strong attack on Fries who had already been suspended from his post for his speech at the Wartburg Festival. Hegel sicked the police on to Fries *not* because of Fries' racism—this is Dr. Avineri's red herring!—but, as Hegel himself explicitly declares, because Fries "did not blush" to express the following wicked ideas in a speech on "The State and the Constitution"! "In the people ruled by a genuine communal spirit, life for the discharge of all public business would come from below; from the people itself; living associations, indissolubly united by the holy chain of friendship, would be dedicated to every single project of popular education and popular service."

Fries' intellectual crime, according to Hegel, is that he dissolves the mighty structure of the State in a brew of "heart, friendship, and inspiration." He is a menace because his philosophy lacks "reverence for law and for an absolute truth exalted above the subjective form of feeling." Since philosophy, Hegel goes on to say, can exist "only in the interest of the state," the government has a right to look into such dangerous ideas. Philosophers, in other words, are to function as members of the ideological police. Not only does Hegel approve of Fries' punishment but seems to be egging the régime on to go further and to imprison him.

The like of Hegel's behavior cannot be found in subsequent philosophical history until the rise of the Soviet Union in which philosophy is also practiced "only in the service of the state." To make matters worse—if that were possible—when a reviewer of the *Rechtsphilosophie* in the *Hallischen Allgemeinen Literaturzeitung* of February 1822, mildly protested against

Hegel's kicking a man already down (*absichtliche Kränkung eines ohnehin gebeugten Mannes. Edel ist ein solches Betragen nicht . . .*), Hegel demanded that the government take action against the paper and the reviewer, Rosenkranz, despite his loyalty to Hegel, has the good grace to be ashamed of Hegel's remarks about Fries and of his attempt to bring the police in to settle philosophical differences. Hegel was unblushingly conscious of the services he was performing for the régime in directing the ideas of the student youth along the right lines. (*Letter to Altenstein,* 3 July 1822.)

Why all this should leave me in Dr. Avineri's eyes a defender of the Wartburg Festival and its windy rhetoric, I cannot fathom. The question is whether the grounds on which Hegel condemned Fries and other participants illustrate a liberal philosophy or its profound absence. According to Avineri, Hegel attacked Fries "because his Wartburg Address was one of the worst demogogic, fanatical, obscurantist, and racialist outbursts of German chauvinism." How false this is Hegel's own words cited above show. There is something amusing about the idea of Hegel attacking anyone as an obscurantist. But not only is Avineri wrong about Hegel but in this instance about Fries, too. The most charitable interpretation of his remarks about Fries is that he has not read Fries' Wartburg Address, *An die deutschen Burschen.* It is a frothy talk about civic equality, truth, and German freedom. It invokes memories of the Battle of Leipzig and declares that the struggle for the liberation of the spirit begun by Luther is continuous with the struggle of the Netherlands and the U.S.A. *There is not a word about the Jews in it.*[1]

Space does not permit adequate discussion of the Wartburg Festival and the complexities of the *Burschenschaft* movement. In effect the meeting was a call for a democratic, unified, constitutional Germany and the participants were persecuted because of this. Only the desperate necessity of bolstering a predetermined thesis and not genuine inquiry could lead someone to believe that the architects of the Holy Alliance persecuted the *Burschenschaft* because it was reactionary. The Wartburg Festival was obviously marked by xenophobic, romantic *Schwärmerei* and the kind of Teutonic high jinks that can be quite dismal. But it could not have been as completely reactionary as Avineri implies. For in addition to burning the works of Professor Schmaltz (a court toady whose views were well suited to his name, the works of von Haller, whom *Hegel* attacked as a reactionary, were also burned. The Nazis, of course, have made bonfires of books completely unrespectable; but the practice was not uncommon among all political groups in the past.

6. Hegel's very *language* is one which no genuine liberal would employ. This is a psychological point but in a political context, where attitudes toward institutions are involved, it is not without significance. The inescapable overtones of language cannot be ignored. That no truly religious man (as Professor Bochenski observes of Ockham) in writing on logic would use, even for purposes of illustration, a blasphemous expression, I am uncertain. But I am confident that no genuine liberal could write of the state as Hegel did. "Man must venerate the State as a secular deity (*Irdisch-Göttliches*)" or "The march of God in the world, that is what the State is." (*Es ist der Gang Gottes in der Welt, dass der Staat ist.*)

7. It is not only Hegel's language but the substance of his position on key issues, too many to enumerate here, which betray his conservatism. For example, his defense of war as necessary for the health of the state; his view that history is the court of last judgment and that therefore every lost cause is an irrational one; his low opinion of freedom of the press and approval of the Carlsbad Decrees; his denigration of a truly representative legislature; his claim that the state has a right to *require* that individuals belong to some church; his view that constitutions are given by history, not made, and that every people gets the constitution it deserves; and his conception of education as "the transformation of the soul," a process by which the individuality of students is reduced to a point where they fit easily into the common cultural mould (a precursory expression of the view of the intellectual as "an engineer of the soul").

No thinker, of course, is all of a piece, and even a liberal is entitled to some conservative prejudices and gaucheries. But although it does not tell us everything about him or about his insights and influence in many different fields, it is hardly an exaggeration to say that with respect to his social and political thought, Hegel is the very model of a small-minded, timid Continental conservative. There is no more reason to regard Hegel as a liberal than Plato as a democrat.

Even without the "external" evidence, an analysis of Hegel's leading ideas, which cannot be given here,[2] will show the essentially conservative strain of his thought. First of all, his theory of *Vernunft* has nothing to do with what is normally understood by "reasonable," even as a term for a family of meanings, and his *Freiheit* is just as foreign to what is normally meant by "freedom" in empirical affairs. The use of intelligence to maximize the possibilities of human freedom to which the philosophy of liberalism has always been committed is precisely what Hegel condemns as dangerous to law and order. He himself makes no bones about his belief that his "logic" is profoundly different "from the current logic elsewhere." The customary logic makes a sharp distinction between validity and history. Hegel's logic is nothing but the morphology of the historical process. In the end it is indistinguishable from a theodicy.

Hegel tries to wriggle out of the quietistic consequences of his identification of the "actual" and the "reasonable" by metaphysical doubletalk about the difference between mere "existence" and "actuality." But no operational indication is given of how to distinguish between what is apparently "actual" and really "actual" except the test of time, because even the apparently actual is logically necessary. Meanwhile, one waits on, and with, the *status quo*. Doctrinally, the only way Hegel escapes from the palpable absurdity of his pronouncements is to convert them into arbitrary tautologies. When the murky clouds of speculation lift, Hegel will always be found to be the philosopher-laureate of the Establishment.

According to Hegel, no one has a right to teach a society or state what it *should* be or to attempt to make the world more reasonable. This is the sin of liberals and reformers, those who always-know-better, who use abstractions as weapons to challenge existing institutions, unaware of the good reasons why things are as they are, and that in criticizing the historical world they are criticizing divine Reason whose cunning is unfathomable to common sense or to understanding, particularly British and French. To talk about the errors and crimes of history, to wonder about what would have happened if some event or action had not occurred, is to be guilty of subjectivism and impiety. For that would be equivalent to giving hints to the divine Spirit on how to improve the world. True piety consists in grasping and accepting the logic of historical development which both explains and justifies what is.

The position is obviously self-defeating since any rebel or reformer could claim to be the instrument of Reason or God, and who is to say to him nay? Hegel, like all conservatives, is not opposed to past revolutions but only those that threaten us in the present. Nor is he opposed to reforms, only to those demanded by the masses. If anything needs to be done, those whom the "World-Spirit" has entrusted with the destinies of the people, either the officialdom or the great men, the Caesars of world-history, will do it. And no matter how they do it they must not be judged by ordinary principles of morality. "Nor must the litany of private virtues—modesty, humility, philanthropy and forbearance be raised against them." Does this sound like Locke, Paine, Jefferson, Bentham, Mill?

One could rest the whole case for the characterisation of Hegel's social philosophy as basically conservative, on his doctrine of *Sittlichkeit*. Hegel has some profoundly true things to say about the extent to which the forms and norms of the individual mind are determined by the institutional culture of society. But he dissolves the individual too much in the system of *Sittlichkeit* (the ethos or ethical use and wont of society). He exaggerates the harmonies and plays down the conflicts in the putative system. The result is that insufficient justice is done to the individual of creative moral insight, to the rebel, prophet, and nonconformist. There is a natural presumption that he is wrong; the bias of age-old experience is against him.

The individual who breaks with the system of *Sittlichkeit* that nurtured him becomes, according to Hegel, not a free individual but no individual at all. He has as much "reality" as a point which is not on a line. He has become an abstraction; a difficulty; a brute negative existence. A highly idealized and unhistorical version of the Greek *polis* seems to be one of the models of Hegel's political thought. He is fond of quoting the ancients to the effect that virtue is living according to the customs of one's own people and community, or in his own words in the *Rechtsphilosophie,* "virtue [is] the individual's simple conformity with the duties of the station to which he belongs . . . he has simply to follow the well-known and explicit rules of his own situation." Woe to a society in which men try to change their station without the guidance of their betters! It is against the order of both Nature and Reason!

It should now be clear why Hegel is much closer to Burke than to Paine and Jefferson. Put a glaze of Reason on Burke's "prejudice" and "prescription," and we get Hegel's *Sittlichkeit.* Burke is wiser about history than Hegel because he is more empirical. There is hardly anything which Hegel's apologists have pleaded in behalf of Hegel's "liberalism" that defenders of Burke have not stressed in clarifying Burke's "conservatism" too.[3]

Dr. Pelczynski makes great ado about a passage in Hegel's *The German Constitution* in which Hegel recognizes the right of the people to participate in government. He implies that I deliberately left this passage out to conceal the fact that Hegel believes in representative institutions. He is mistaken. The point of the matter is *how* the people are to be represented and the power of the assembly with respect to monarchy. In one sense "representative" institutions existed even under absolutist régimes. We must always ask: who selected the deputies, and what powers did they have? And if they are elected, how broad is the electoral base? Hegel's *Rechtsphilosophie* as well as his essay on "The English Reform Bill" makes emphatically clear how strongly he is opposed to *popular* representative responsible assemblies. The reason I did not interpret as Dr.

Pelczynski did the long passage quoted by him from the *German Constitution* is the sentence that follows immediately after the passage, and which is part of the same paragraph. It reads: *"Most German states have representation of this kind"* (my italics). In other words, the representation advocated by Hegel, which, according to Dr. Pelczynski, proves that Hegel is a liberal, was the kind that already existed in most German states of the time. But most German states of the time were absolutist! We would not dream of referring to them as organized on liberal, no less democratic, lines. No wonder Dr. Pelczynski left that sentence out. For it reinforces the point that I made in my original article, that for all his talk about participation, politically, Hegel was more inclined to increase the power of royal rulers than the power of the people.

I come finally to the question of nationalism. Here I am at fault in not qualifying more carefully the sense in which I characterized Hegel as a nationalist. My hypothesis concerning the genesis of Hegel's philosophical system is that it was inspired by his desire to counteract or "purify" false ideas of freedom, French and German, which stood in the way of German *unification.* He was not a nationalist in the chauvinistic, expansionist sense. He could sometimes poke fun at German traits. By the time he criticized the agitation for German unification by the *Burschenschaften,* he had already developed his system. His criticism of that movement was due to his conservatism—his conservatism was more pronounced than his nationalism—to his loyalty to the Prussian State, and to his own cautious and fearful temperament. In his letters to Creuzer and Niethammer, he writes, complainingly:

I am almost 50 years old and have spent 30 of them in this constantly stormy time of fear and hope. I hoped sometime to be shed of them. But now I see the situation will continue, yes, in certain dark hours it seems to one to be growing worse. (30 October 1819.)
You know I am on the one hand, a fearful (*ängstlicher*) man, on the other, I love peace; and it is no comfort to see every year

a thunderstorm blow up even when I am convinced that at most a few drops of passing rain will strike me. (9 June 1821.)

One could say of the nationalist movement that, like the romantic movement, it contained mystical, promethean, and demonic elements. But of Hegel's nationalism one could say what could never have been said of romanticism, it was a *philistine* nationalism.

The early years of German nationalism are complicated because it was a response to the excesses of the French Revolution and yet profoundly influenced by it in hopes that some of its driving spirit would lead to a better and freer Germany. Roughly three groups existed in Germany—those who defended the semi-feudal *status quo;* those who looked toward the unification and liberalization of Germany; those who wanted just enough gradual reforms from above to forestall revolution on the French model. Hegel was of the last group and originally in favor of national unification but so fearful of the principles and slogans of freedom when used by the *Burschenschaften* that he played it safe and threw in his public lot with the officials of the enlightened bureaucratic Prussian police state, not all of whose actions, in the privacy of his study, he approved. He feared that the popular German movement for freedom would lead to the same results in Germany as in France where, as he put it, "it was as underdeveloped and in its abstraction that it was there applied to actuality; and to make abstractions hold good in actuality means to destroy actuality. *The fanaticism which characterised the freedom which was put into the hands of the people was frightful.*" (*History of Philosophy,* Vol 3, my italics.)

Dr. Avineri admits that Hegel was strongly for national unification when he wrote *The German Constitution* (1802), but interprets this as evidence of Hegel's liberalism, whereas I interpret his desire for a united Germany as originally a patriotic reaction to the terrible things the French troops were doing in Germany. Even Haym acknowledges Hegel's strong reaction against the political humiliations of the day but unfairly takes him to task because although Hegel called for a new Germany, he worked to accomplish it, not by action, but by metaphysical thought. "Unable to carry out his ideal into reality, he transforms reality into his ideal." Avineri vastly exaggerates "Hegel's hostile attitude to the German anti-French insurrection in 1813." He praises it in his *Antrittsrede* at Heidelberg and again at Berlin. To be sure, Hegel is often fed up with the excesses not only of the French troops but of all the allied troops, and especially the burden of quartering Russian and Prussian soldiers. His most extended comment on Napoleon's surrender is his letter to Niethammer (29 April 1814) in which he proudly claims that he had already predicted the entire course of events *before* the battle of Jena and cites from the *Phänomenologie* as evidence. In other words, Napoleon, that "self-destructive genius," is seen, not as a liberator, but despite some good works as the final executor of the terror of reason unleashed by the Revolution. That Hegel admired Napoleon as a great historical figure without approving of French depredations in Germany is not inconsistent. It is not even necessary to endorse Plamenatz' statement that, "Hegel admired Napoleon as perhaps only a German is capable of admiring a conqueror of his country." Most of the crowned heads of Europe had the same ambivalent feelings toward him. Napoleon had murdered more people than Robespierre but they recognized in him the upstart who would have liked to be one of them.

Although Avineri admits that Hegel called for the unification of Germany in his *German Constitution,* he seeks to dismiss this as incidental. "What Hegel criticises is the *absence of any sort of political authority in Germany.*" This is an absurd retort, for the point is that political authority could be established *only* by unification. Far from being peripheral that is the central point. For only such unification could prevent the dismemberment and continued humiliation of Germany at French hands about which Hegel is so eloquent. The evidence that Germany is no longer a state, according to Hegel, is the unsuccessful way in which it has waged war against the French invader because "a multitude of human beings can only call itself a state if it be united for the common defence of the entirety of its property." Because Hegel's motives for demanding the unification of Germany were different from those of the romantic, proto-racist troglodytes of his time is not a valid ground for denying the fact that he made such a demand or its significance for the genesis of his philosophy.

In saying that Hegel would have welcomed the Bismarckian unification—as he would have opposed the German Revolution of 1848 and supported Hugenberg's *Deutschnationale Partei* in 1932 (not the Nazis)—I thought I was saying the obvious. Even T. L. Haering, than whom there is no more pious admirer of Hegel, observes "that Bismarck to a large extent realised Hegel's ideas has often been noted" (*Hegel: Sein Wollen und Sein Werk,* Bk. II, p. 337), although Haering doubts that Bismarck, since his work did not endure, was a true Hegelian. But as far as the unification of Germany is concerned, all one need do is to read Hegel's extravagant praise of Machiavelli, to see that Bismarck in this respect (and not in this respect alone) fits Hegel's conception of a great statesman and patriot perfectly—blood, iron, fraud, passion, "ideals," and all. In saying that Hegel was a philosopher of the Bismarckian (and Wilhelmian) Establishment, I was *not* referring to Rosenkranz' book or to Hegel as a German national cultural treasure on the order of Goethe. If Dr. Avineri had read what I wrote with more care, he would have noted that I referred to Hegel as the *Nationalstaatsphilosoph,* not as *Nationalphilosoph* (and saved himself the needless trouble of abusing Rosenkranz). I am well aware that Hegel's technical philosophy was in almost total eclipse from 1840 to about 1910, when Dilthey and Windelband sparked the renewal of interest in Hegel's speculative thought; but Hegel's *political* philosophy, his *organic* theory of the state, his conception of *war* flourished. It remained the most influential political philosophy in Germany up to World War I.

One need not accept the exaggerated claims made by Heller in his *Hegel und der Nationale Machtstaatsgedanke in Deutschland* (1921) that Bismarck himself was influenced by

Hegel, even though he couldn't read him, to recognize that Droysen, Duncker, Lasson, and especially Rössler, who was close to Bismarck, all avowed disciples of Hegel, exercised not only theoretical but immense practical influence. Fredrich Meinecke in his *Weltbürgertum und Nationalstaat* (1919) claims that the three men who contributed most to liberating Germany from its unpolitical romantic ideas and paved the way for the realistic politics of the pre-World War I era were Hegel, Ranke, and Bismarck. The socialist, J. Plenge (in his *1789 and 1914*) contrasted Kant as the leading exponent of the ideas of the French Revolution, abstract liberty, with Hegel as the philosopher of "organised liberty." "The opposition of the ideas of 1789 and 1914 in philosophy is the opposition between Kant and Hegel . . . between the atomic will and the well-coordinated partial self (*eingegliedertes Teil-Ich*)."

Dr. Avineri takes issue with my statement that Hegel was a nationalist from the very beginning of his career. I was referring to the *Constitution of Germany,* originally written in 1799. With a great show of correcting me, Avineri quotes a passage from the second part of Hegel's *The Positivity of the Christian Religion,* written in 1796, in which he repudiates the old German imagery as irrelevant to "our day." But Avineri remains tactfully silent about the fact that the paragraph concludes with the sentence, "Is Judea, then, the Teuton's fatherland? This question is asked in connection with the chief point of the essay: "How did Christianity Conquer Paganism?" Hegel's answer is that when the ideal of the state or nation disappears a people looks for other-worldly salvation.

> Greek and Roman religion was a religion for free peoples only, and with the loss of freedom, its significance and strength were also bound to perish. . . .
> The idea of his country or his state was the invisible, and higher reality for which the individual strove. . . . Confronted by this idea his own individuality vanished.

The young Hegel rages almost like Nietzsche against Christianity.

Christianity has emptied Valhalla, filled the sacred groves, extirpated the national imagery as a shameful superstition, as a devilish poison, and given us instead the imagery of a nation whose climate, laws, culture, and interests are strange to us. . . . Except perhaps for Luther in the eyes of the Protestants, what heroes could we have, *we who were never a nation? Who could be our Theseus?* [My italics.]

Hegel feels strongly about a German state and fatherland and makes unmistakably clear what is necessary to get it. One must fight for it! Christianity triumphed over Rome when "passive resistance" took the place of military service. Only when the Jews were subjugated by foreign nations, Hegel reminds us, were they offered a Messiah, but "they very soon discovered their ineffective messianic hopes and took up arms." They fought to remain a state! With an eye obviously on Germany, he adds: *"A nation to which this is a matter of indifference will soon cease to be a nation."* Hegel praises the Jews very highly for going down fighting to preserve their national independence. The Jews "would stand above the Greeks and Romans, whose cities outlived their politics, *if the sense of what a nation may do for its independence were not too foreign to us. . . ."* There is a continuity between what I called Hegel's nationalism in the *Constitution of Germany* and some elements in his *Early Theological Writings.*

In conclusion, I see no reason to alter my view that Hegel was a national, conservative thinker. I believe this throws light on the genesis of his system. The validity, however, of Hegel's many insights into the nature of human culture is independent of his politics and personality, neither of which is very admirable.

NOTES

1. Fries *had* published a tract against the Jews but *not* on religious or racialist grounds, Like some other liberal and socialist thinkers who ignored the cruel social conditions which compelled Jews to engage in commerce, Fries attacked them for their alleged economic role. In defending this calamitous

lapse from otherwise liberal positions—Principal Knox refers to Fries as "an ultra-liberal thinker"—he wrote: "I really want Judaism to be reformed and abolished as a commercial caste (*Handelskaste*) so that the Jews can participate as fully qualified citizens of the State. . . ." (*Nachlass,* edited by E. Henke, p. 158.)

2. I have touched briefly on them in my essay, "Hegel and the Perspective of Liberalism," in *A Hegel Symposium,* edited by D. C. Travis (University of Texas Press, 1962).

3. From a collection of Burke's writings nearest at hand, I quote the following editorial remarks: "Because Burke is a conservative, it is sometimes falsely assumed that he was a natural enemy of all revolution. That is not so. Burke's attack on the French revolution was not . . . a defence of history against reason. He was perhaps above all else a defender of reason. What he hated was rationalism . . . abstractions." And so on. (Bredvold and Ross, *The Philosophy of Burke,* University of Michigan Press, 1960).

III Two Solos

9 *Hegel and Nationalism*

SHLOMO AVINERI

I

Hegel was a resident of Jena when the Battle of Jena, a shattering defeat for Prussia, took place.[1] On October 13, 1806, the day on which the French entered the town and deployed for the engagement fought the next day, Hegel wrote to his friend Niethammer:

> As I wrote to you earlier, all of us here wish the French victory and success. The Prussians are suffering the defeats they deserve. . . . This morning I saw the Emperor Napoleon, that World Soul (*diese Weltseele*), riding through the town to a parade. It's a marvelous feeling to see such a personality dominating the entire world from horseback. . . . He is capable of doing anything. How wonderful he is![2]

This paper appeared originally in *The Review of Politics,* October 1962. It was thus published before the second debate, above.

Three months later in a letter to another friend, Zelmann, Hegel summed up the historical lesson of the Battle of Jena: "There is no better proof than the events occuring before our eyes, that culture is triumphing over barbarism and the intellect over spirit-less mind."[3]

Hegel was writing this while Fichte was agitating, first in Königsberg and then in Berlin, against the French. What Fichte preached in his *Addresses to the German Nation* in 1807–8, he fulfilled in 1813, when he joined the nationalist university volunteer corps to fight against the French and died in that service. On his part Hegel, who had become headmaster of a Gymnasium in Nuremberg, remained loyal to his pro-French, anti-German orientation. Commenting on Nuremberg's liberation from French occupation, Hegel wrote, once again to Niethammer, on May 2, 1813: "Several hundred thousand Cossacks, Bashkirs and Prussian patriots have seized the city."[4]

Several days later he alluded to a nightmare his wife had had concerning the "Cossacks, Prussians and other savage troops."[5] In another letter, dated December 23, 1813, he mocked the enthusiasm of the nationalist students over the liberation: "Liberation? Liberation from what? They talk a great deal here about Liberation. If I ever see one *liberated* person with my own eyes, I shall fall to the ground and prostrate myself before him."[6]

When echoes of Napoleon's final defeat reached Nuremberg, Hegel exclaimed: "Our great Napoleon—who would ever have believed that this would be his end?"[7] And when the German romantic nationalistic movement agitated for the establishment of a united Germany subsequent to liberation, Hegel rejoiced at the outcome of the Congress of Vienna, which perpetuated the numerous small states of Germany.[8] In an essay on the constitutional struggle in Württemberg, Hegel wrote (1816): "The vain idea known as the German Reich has disappeared."[9]

When the nationalist students' fraternities (the *Burschenschaften*) stirred up the Wartburg pilgrimage in 1817, and

Hegel's colleague and intellectual opponent at Berlin University, Jakob Friedric Fries, delivered his famous speech at the rally, in which he visualized a unified and liberated Germany, Hegel devoted most of the Introduction to his *Philosophy of Right* to an attack on the Fries School and its subjectivism. While the extreme Burschenschaft, Teutonia, wrote into its statutes the aim of a Pan-German consciousness in place of loyalty to the individual German states, Hegel pointed out that those who sought to establish in Germany political unity beyond and above the existing boundaries understood nothing of politics or history.[10] When student fraternities refused to accept Jewish students as members, Hegel demanded the granting of full equality of political and civic rights to the Jews, since "a man counts as a man in virtue of his manhood alone, not because he is a Jew, Catholic, Protestant, German, Italian, etc."[11]

As a final example of Hegel's criticism of German nationalism, his hostility to the Aryan concept may be cited. F. von Schlegel's book, *The Language and Wisdom of the Indians,* appearing in the twenties, first expounded the *Aryan* view in Germany arguing for a national and racial affinity between the Germans and the Indians on the basis of the linguistic relationship between Sanskrit and Old Gothic. Schlegel was the first to coin the phrase, "the Aryan Peoples." In the *Introduction to the Philosophy of History* Hegel ridiculed these assumptions about the existence of an ancient "original" Indo-European *Ur-Volk*. He stated that any attempt to draw political and historical conclusions from linguistic evidence meant the conversion of science into mythology.[12]

II

The obvious question emerging from this survey of Hegel's actual attitudes toward the different political and cultural manifestations of German nationalism is: How did it happen that a thinker who expressed himself in such unequivocal terms against the German national movement over a long period of years came to be regarded, as he still is today, as the intellectual and spiritual father of German nationalism? How did it come about that the man who so harshly criticized the first signs of the Aryan racial doctrine should be regarded as the founder of German nationalism and racialism by a scholar like Karl Popper;[13] or that a thinker who opposed every attempt at political unity in Germany should be considered by Hermann Heller to be the first exponent of the modern nationalist state?[14] It is easy to cite a long list of scholars who hold the same view as to the close connection between Hegel and German nationalism and racialist Nazism.[15]

It is of crucial importance to observe that this view of Hegel is a new and fundamentally revolutionary one. The Germans of the nineteenth century, who knew Hegel in the context of the German political reality of his period, saw him as utterly hostile to nationalism. Such, for example, is the view of Rudolf Haym, the nationalist historian of the Frankfurt Assembly of 1848.[16] Writing in 1857, he denounced Hegel as the foe equally of liberalism and of German nationalism. Haym saw Hegel's attachment to Prussia as a proof of his antinationalism as well as of his antiliberalism. In his lectures of 1897 Treitschke, also, referred to Hegel in a rather condescending manner: Hegel did not, and could not, understand the nationalist connection between the *Volk* and the state.[17]

How did the evaluation of Hegel come to be altered in such a radical way during recent decades?

Three complementary answers may be suggested:

1. The Hegelian school in attempting to emerge from its political isolation and to become part of the German national movement of the fifties drew nearer to nationalism and took to interpreting Hegel in a nationalist spirit. This is rather obvious, for example, in Karl Rosenkranz's expositions of his master's doctrine. Rosenkranz wrote three books on Hegel. The first, *The Life of Hegel* published in 1844, made no specific mention of his subject's stand on the national question. The second, dating from 1858, was a rejoinder to Haym's accusations

(*Apologie Hegels gegen Dr. R. Haym*). Here Rosenkranz claimed for the first time that Hegel was not alien to German nationalism. The very title of the third book, published in the significant year 1870, revealed how far in assessing his master's doctrines Rosenkranz had been influenced by his own *Zeitgeist:* it was called *Hegel as a German National Philosopher* (*Hegel als deutscher Nationalphilosoph*)—a title completely inconceivable twenty or thirty years earlier.

2. The *volte-face* which occurred in the role of Prussia in German nationalism in the nineteenth century did much to confuse the meaning of Hegel's so-called "Prussianism." Up to Bismarck's time, Prussia's attitude to German unification was extremely hostile and in 1857 Haym could denounce Hegel for being antiliberal and antinational *on the ground of his Prussian connections.* Bismarck's policy, by directing Prussia to become the instrument of German unification, completely changed the image of Prussia in European thought: while still remaining antiliberal, it became utterly nationalistic in outlook. Thus Hegel's Prussianism was given not only an antiliberal connotation, but also a nationalistic one. This is clearly an anachronism, achieved by projecting the image of the Prussia of 1870 (or, perhaps, even of 1914–1918) back upon 1820. This was carried to its extreme by Popper, who looked on Hegel as the "servant" of the Prussian court *and* the prophet of German nationalism at the same time: these are mutually exclusive political orientations in the context of 1820, but Popper had the Bismarckian image of Prussia before him and read backwards from it to the Prussia of the Congress of Vienna.

3. The fragmentary publication of Hegel's manuscript "The Constitution of Germany" (*Die Verfassung Deutschlands*) did much to create a twisted image of Hegel's attitude toward nationalism. Extracts from his unpublished and unknown manuscript, written during 1801–2, were first published by Rosenkranz when, in his controversy with Haym, he was trying to prove Hegel's nationalism. In this essay Hegel offered an explanation of the collapse of the German states before the

French onslaught. Hegel attributed the collapse mainly to the feudal structure of the decrepit Holy Roman Empire. He tried to find a way in which the balance of power in Europe could be redressed by establishing a strong Central European power within the framework of the *historical* Reich, but only as a political unit, without national or ethnic-linguistic connotations. The essay trailed off on a rather pessimistic note when he expressed the opinion that the attempt would probably not succeed. Even the name given to the essay is not Hegel's, who left it without a title. The essay runs to some 140 pages, and the extracts published by Rosenkranz do not exceed a tenth of the total. This carefully biased fragmentary publication created around 1850 the impression that Hegel was advocating something like German unification, and readers were unable to verify this impression which would have been exploded had the work been published in its entirety. This fragmentary acquaintance served as a basis for a popular exposition of Hegel's views in the significant year 1870. The work, written by Karl Köstlin of Tübingen, treated Hegel as the philosopher of the national German states.[18] This book was largely responsible for the popular image of Hegel in Wilhelmian Germany, and to prove his point Köstlin relied heavily on the extracts quoted by Rosenkranz—*without ever having seen the full text of the original for himself.*

The full text of the "Constitution of Germany" was published for the first time in 1893 by Georg Mollat. But by that time the public image of Hegel had already been so wholly transformed by the popular expositions of the fragmentary text, that the publication of the full text did not change much in the interpretation of Hegel's position. Scholars and publicists went on quoting the familiar passages and, though their pagination referred to Mollat's edition, they appear not to have looked afresh at the whole essay. The first one who based his interpretation of the essay on the whole text was Franz Rosenweig whose study only appeared after the First World War. And he overlooked a key passage because it did not square with the established image of Hegel; it is the passage in which Hegel remarked about the characteristic of the modern states:

In our times, there is no need for integration or unity in the states as far as custom, tradition, culture, and language are concerned. . . . The dialects of many provinces of France and England differ from the dominant tongue. . . . In Wales and the Hebrides English is not spoken at all. . . . The Austrian and Russian monarchs do not even know how many languages are spoken in their states—and precisely their states are models of the modern state, whose integration arises . . . from the spirit and unity of a common political consciousness.[19]

It is not surprising that this passage, and others as well, were simply overlooked by those who tried to find in Hegel the philosopher of nationalism.

Thus Hegel came to be interpreted as a German nationalist by two absolutely opposed political traditions. First, the German national movement of the end of the last century claimed Hegel as part and parcel of the German heritage on nationalist terms; secondly, liberal Anglo-Saxons maintained during the Nazi regime that Hegel's antiliberalism must involve extreme nationalism—and went about tearing Hegel to pieces on those two grounds alike. It is significant that in the nineteenth century none of the English Hegelians ever mentioned any possibility of a nationalist connotation of Hegel's philosophy, though they were aware of his political *étatist* tenets.

It is true, of course, that Hegel would never have been interpreted in a nationalist vein had there not been similarities between some of his expressions, if not opinions, and those of nationalist thinkers. As for the affinities of Hegel's terminology with that of nationalism, the main point of overlapping seems to be Hegel's use of the terms *Volksgeist* and *Volk,* which held a central position in German nationalism itself. It may, then, be helpful, to ascertain Hegel's meaning in using those terms, and to relate it to the common usage of German nationalism, in an effort to determine whether the meaning of Hegel's term can be interpreted in a nationalist light.

The inquiry will be conducted on three levels: the concept of *Volksgeist* in Hegel's early writings will be presented; a comparison will be drawn between Hegel's usage of the term and the meaning attributed to it by Savigny's School of German Historical Jurisprudence; and finally the meaning of this term in Hegel's *Philosophy of History* will be examined.

III

Hegel's early writings were first published by Hermann Nohl in 1907, and down to 1948 remained untranslated into any other language. The fact that they were completely unknown in the nineteenth century and are still very little known compared with his later writings, has certainly done a lot to influence the general image of Hegel's thought and its development.

These writings reveal Hegel's spiritual development while he was gradually liberating himself from Kantian philosophy and slowly working out his own conceptual system. Parallel to this, he was also gradually freeing himself from deep Herderian influences which must be considered in order to find out the significances of the concept of *Volk* to Hegel.

The first of Hegel's early writings, written in 1796,[a] is called *The Positivity of the Christian Religion (Die Positivität der christlichen Religion)*. This is Hegel's sharpest attack on Christianity. In it he combined Kant's outlook in the realm of ethics with outlooks derived from Herder in the cultural sphere. He rebuked Christianity for being a "positive" religion, that is, based on normative, positive, and institutionalized commandments. These are external to the individual's self-consciousness and constitute moral coercion, as they prevent him from exercising his autonomous moral decision.

The essay is a panegyric of the Greek popular religion of paganism (*Volksreligion*), contrasted with Christianity. In strict Herderian terms, Hegel saw religion, as well as morality and art, as a manifestation of the people's spirit (*Volksgeist*). Every people has its own *Volksgeist,* incorporating a unity of life which is peculiar to it. This appears in the spiritual wholeness of the individual, who merges his entire being into the spirit of

---

[a] Actually, in 1795. It is "the first" only in the English edition. The German volume contains some earlier fragments on folk religion. w.k.

his people. Following Herder's "Christianity and the National Religions," Hegel stated that every people has its own specific sociocultural institutions corresponding to its national character. This also explains historically, according to Hegel, the appearance of Christ against the background of "the miserable situation of the Jewish nation."[20] This occurred because the divine legislation of Moses, accompanied as it was by numerous and burdensome statutory commandments, converted the Jewish people into a nation of recluses, priding itself on its servile obedience to the Law. When a foreign power, Rome, intruded into this closed system, imposing upon the Jews subjection to an *outside political order,* the hermetic character of Jewish religious exclusivism was impaired. Out of this tension there arose the messianic belief—and Hegel was one of the first moderns to interpret the Messiah as an embodiment of the national consciousness of the Jewish people. The Messiah, "girdled with might as Jehova's plenipotentiary, was to rebuild the Jewish state from its foundations."[21]

This *political* interpretation of early Jewish Messianism is a consequence of the entire Herderian explanation of the historical background of the appearance of Jesus. It is a consequence of the uniqueness of Judaism: the Mosaic religion cannot coexist with any other link to the external world, Hegel maintained, and as Judaism and foreign rule are irreconcilable, the reconstitution of the Jewish state becomes a necessity arising from the *peculiar* (and rather heavily criticized from Hegel's side) character of Judaism. *This is not a universal demand for political independence as a prerequisite for every people.* Only the Jewish people, because of its peculiar and hermetic religion requires itself as "a people dwelling unto itself." Political independence, therefore, is not the historical norm but the deviation, which excludes Israel from the generality of the historical process itself.

In another work, dating from the same year, "On the Difference between the Imaginative Religion of the Greeks and Christian Positive Religion" (*Unterschied zwischen griechischer Phantasie und christlicher positiver Religion*), Hegel sought the reason for the triumph of Christianity over paganism. This essay was written in a spirit similar to that of the work just discussed. But the conclusions deducible from it regarding our inquiry are somewhat different. Hegel ascribed the triumph of Christianity not to any rational superiority on its side, but to a certain prior revolution in habits and cultural outlook. His words strike a very typical note in 1796, and the mature Hegel may already be seen between the lines:

> Great revolutions which strike the eye at a glance must have been preceded by a still and secret revolution in the spirit of the age (*Zeitgeist*), a revolution not visible to every eye, especially imperceptible to contemporaries, and as hard to discern as to describe in words. It is lack of acquaintance with this spiritual revolution which makes the resulting changes astonishing.[22]

What was this inner revolution which enabled and preconditioned the spread of Christianity? It was the transition from the free city-state to the Empire. The pagan religion was the religion of free citizens: the gods are the creation of their imagination in the same way as the *polis* is the creation of their consciousness. The *polis* is the eternal essence in which every citizen sees the continuation of his life even after his physical death. Thus pagan Greek religion could be content with gods replete with human failures, because the eternal and transcendental was engraved on the inner soul of each citizen. But the servility imposed by the Empire needed another sort of deity, and Christianity, itself, according to Hegel, as product of servitude, offered itself to a population degraded by fear and terror. The Christian deity was not produced by free will, as the Empire was no longer the voluntary republican *polis*. Prayer replaced will and this corrupt generation could without difficulty accept a religion based on the moral corruption of mankind, expressed in the Christian doctrine of sin. Sin itself became a religious value, immanent in human nature—and the Emperors viewed favorably a religion which would divert men's attention from their actual sociopolitical conditions to a salvation to be found in heaven. The very debasement of life became a sanctified value.

Behind this fierce republican and anti-Christian tirade, a new meaning of the *Volksgeist* can be seen emerging. As in the previous work, religion appears as one of the manifestations of the *Volksgeist*. The concept itself is not primarily spiritual-cultural but turns out to be mainly political in its essence: the measure of political liberty, the methods of political and social institutionalization are no longer mere *phenomena* of a hidden, rather vague *Volksgeist* working from behind the scene—they are its very *essence*. The political sphere becomes dominant in determining the religious experience and the sociocultural attitudes and values. Thus, the *Zeitgeist* of the Roman imperial period differed from the republican not because the *Volksgeist* changed: the *Volksgeist* changed because of the transformation of political institutions, arising from a new social class and/or geographical structure. Thus the "totality" of the Herderian *Volksgeist* became highly politicized, probably under the impact of the French Revolution. Perhaps even more important, the *Volksgeist* became more of a descriptive than a genetic term.

With this in mind, the question of political independence raised once more by Hegel in connection with the Jewish nation (and it is not raised by him in any other connection at that period) may be considered. In a rather long and involved passage, Hegel held:

Similarly, so long as the Jewish state found spirit and strength enough in itself for the maintenance of its independence, the Jews seldom, or, as many hold, never, had recourse to the expectation of a Messiah. Not until they were subjugated by foreign nations, not until they had a sense of their impotence and weakness, do we find them burrowing in their sacred books for a consolation of that kind. Then, when they were offered a Messiah who did not fulfil their political expectations, they thought it worth toiling to insure that their state should still remain a state; a nation to which this is a matter of indifference will soon cease to be a nation. They very soon discarded their ineffective messianic hopes and took up arms. . . . In history and the judgement of nations they would stand alongside the Carthaginians and Saguntines, and above the Greeks and Romans, whose cities outlived their polities, if the sense of what a nation may do for its independence were not too foreign to us. . . .[23]

The impulse for independence on the part of the Jews is no longer here explained by the *unique* character of Jewish religion: it appears as a *universal* need, in that intriguing remark scribbled by Hegel on the margin of the original manuscript: "A nation to which this is a matter of indifference will soon cease to be a nation." Is this really a demand in the spirit of modern nationalism?

Hardly so, if it be read within the context of Hegel's essay. It is not the national independence of modern nations that Hegel is referring to, but the political independence of ancient city-states. In an essay in which political values are dominant, the existence of a *political organization* as such is conceived as absolutely necessary to the existence of intellectual and spiritual life. Thus, the Greek *polis* lost its spiritual life following its political subjection—*a subjection which was not necessarily a national one.* A unit which is no longer a political unit in the sense of having its own political institutions and of embodying the will of its citizens, is no longer a social unit at all: it becomes part of another unit, which has engulfed it. That Hegel does not mean national units in any modern sense, but the existence of a state as such as a preliminary condition to cultural life, is evident from the examples adduced of Carthage and Saguntum. Being a people means being organized in a political framework—this is the principle by which *Volk* is defined, here as well as in Hegel's later political writings. This is very similar to Rousseau's *peuple.* Later Hegel wrote about a Prussian *Volk* or a Bavarian *Volk,* etc., because those *states* did exist.

But this is not the last phase of the gradual but significant transformations of Hegel's *Volksgeist.* In the last work belonging to his early period, *The Spirit of Christianity and Its Fate,* written in 1799, the atmosphere is completely different. Under the influence of Hölderlin and possibly also Schlegel, Hegel switched over from rationalistic criticism of Christianity to Christian mysticism, [b] searching for a speculative expression for his religious experiences. As this development is beyond the scope of the present study, it can only be pointed out that thereafter Hegel considered himself a devout Christian, [c] although he never fully agreed with the accepted theological justification of doctrinal terms and his Lutheranism is certainly open to criticism on theological grounds. In this essay, however, Hegel presented Christianity as a blending of Judaism, with its austere commandments, and of Hellenism, consisting here mainly in the cult of beauty and aesthetic experience. According to Hegel, those two qualities require each other in order to create the synthesis of *psyche* (soul) and *physis* (nature).

This is, of course, an obvious romanticization of Christianity, and consequently the Jewish and Greek *Volksgeister* involved cannot any longer be considered as *historical* entities. What Hegel meant here when he referred to Greek or Hebrew spirit has nothing to do with the *actual* Greeks or Hebrews: it is an abstraction of a quality, of a philosophical idea, placed rather arbitrarily by Hegel into a historical reality. The references are no longer to concrete manifestations of any historical phenomenon, a people or a culture, but to the realization of metaphysical ideas ("beauty," "morality," etc.). The concept of *Volksgeist* had in effect become void of all content ascribable to it as a tangibly historical entity.

But before Hegel reached this ultimate reconciliation with Christianity, he wrote, apparently while staying in Berne in 1797, a passage sometimes referred to as "Is Judea, then, the Teutons' Fatherland" (*Ist denn Judäa der Tuiskonen Vaterland?*). Most characteristically, in their fullest form this passage expresses the Herderian ideas of *Volksgeist*—while dialectically refuting them and going beyond them.

Initially Hegel stated that every people possesses its own

[b] This is Kroner's interpretation in his long introduction to Knox's translation. It has been criticized in detail by Kaufmann. See *From Shakespeare to Existentialism,* Chapter 8. W.K.
[c] See the preceding footnote. W.K.

traditions and fantasies about gods, angels, demons, and heroes; they are transmitted from generation to generation, constituting the sociopolitical and cultural heritage. The ancient Germanic tribes possessed such a tradition—but it was destroyed by Christianity:

> Christianity has emptied Valhalla, felled the sacred groves, extirpated the national imagery as a shameful superstition, as a devilish poison, and given us instead the imagery of a nation whose climate, laws, culture, and interests are stranger to us and whose history has no connection whatever with our own. A David or a Solomon lives in our popular imagination, but our own country's heroes slumber in learned history books. . . .[24]

This looks as if it were a preliminary to a plea on Herderian lines to resuscitate the German *Ur-Mythos*. But dialectically Hegel proceeded to attack what he calls the "phoney Germanic literature," which tried to put new life into old Teutonic traditions. This sort of literature, very much connected with Klopstock's name, is severely criticized by Hegel:

> But this imagery is not that of Germans today. The project of restoring to a nation an imagery once lost was always doomed to failure. . . . The old German imagery has nothing in our day to connect or adapt itself to; it stands as cut off from the whole circle of our ideas, opinions, and beliefs, and is as strange to us as the imagery of Ossian or of India.[25]

Hegel never reversed this verdict on the German national Romantic attempt to revive the old mythology. Over thirty years later, when lecturing on aesthetics at Berlin University, he had this to say about Klopstock and his school:

> Very prominent in Klopstock is the consciousness of the fatherland. As a poet he sensed the need for a rooted mythology, whose names and forms should compose in themselves a solid base for fantasy. . . . It may be said that out of national pride Klopstock tried to revive the mythology of Wothan, Herta and the rest. All he succeeded in doing was that the *names* of the Gods took on German instead of Greek forms, and no more. Klopstock attained to no greater influence and objective actuality than a man

who endeavors to argue that the Imperial Diet of Regensburg can constitute the ideal of our present national existence. *Those Gods who have sunk into oblivion will always remain hollow and false,* and a good deal of hypocrisy is needed to pretend that this fantasy is reconcilable with intelligence and with the present consciousness of the nation.[26]

To sum up: Hegel used Herder's term *Volksgeist,* but with a connotation, which excludes any interpretation that he favored a return to the Germanic *Ur-Volk.* In Hegel's thought the *Volksgeist* underwent a profound process of rationalization; it is not the origin of the historical phenomena, but is really the outcome of them, and thus tautological with it. It cannot be interpreted in the spirit of national and romantic myth. The self-same myths which acted as a driving force in the development of revived German national consciousness were those later transformed into the racialist and pagan Nazi ideology. Hegel's historiosophical concepts, on the other hand, were not conceived as a means of romanticizing the present in the image of the past. For, as Heraclitus said, one cannot step twice into the same river and Hegel the dialectician always remained hostile to any attempt to revive the past: this was his point of view when he was a young private tutor in Berne and remanied his belief when in his later years he served as Professor of Philosophy in Berlin.

IV

The second level of our investigation is concerned with the respective meanings attached to the term *Volksgeist* in Hegel and in the writing of the German Historical School of Jurisprudence, founded by Savigny and Puchta.

In the usage of the Historical School the concept served as a lever for the German nationalist consciousness to identify itself with what was thought to have been the institutions of ancient German law. This self-identification reached its peak in the attempt to do away with the existing rational European legal system and reconstruct what was conceived to be ancient German-national tribal law, thus replacing "formal" Roman law by "popular primeval" German justice.[27]

The question here posed is whether the term *Volksgeist* had the same meaning in Hegel's writings as the one it received in the Historical School. The various scholars who have engaged in this line of inquiry agree on the fundamental facts relating to the actual use of the term:[28] the concept of *Volksgeist* reached the Historical School through Hegel. Savigny used it only after it had come to him through Puchta who was Hegel's pupil. But this is not yet an answer to the question, whether the meaning of the concept is identical.

In order to examine this, it is necessary to determine what the Historical School meant in using the term, then to ascertain whether the same meaning can be ascribed to the term in Hegel's writings, and finally to examine in what measure Hegel himself actually took issue with Savigny's school.

According to Savigny's *On Our Generation's Legislative Task* (1813) law stands in an organic connection with the nation's character. The nature of law constitutes the inner essence of the nation and stems from its history, for every nation has its own particular laws and customs in accordance with its particular and unique spirit. The reason and origin of the law are found in that layer of national consciousness which also produces language and custom. Law lives in the nation's original (*ursprünglich*) consciousness. It is created by unconscious historical forces, not by the conscious will of the formal legislator. Just as the grammarian never determines the laws of language, but describes them as they exist and function, so the legislator merely describes the prevailing procedures in the life of society. In accordance with German historical legal consciousness, Savigny stated that the legislator merely gives external formalization to contents already inherent in the national character. He is no more than the external representative of the *Volksgeist* which does its silent and secret work in concealment, in the bosom of the historical process itself.

In Puchta's works the romanticization of the concept of law goes deeper and further into the political sphere; as law is the product of an unconscious and primeval national force, so is the state, which is not the outcome of rational, conscious will, but a product of dormant historical forces. Neither law nor the state is open to rational criticism or argument. Law and the state, according to the Historical School, always are what they should be. Positive legislation and conscious general codification—insofar as they reflect the *Volksgeist* and the existing legal values inherent in the people—are superfluous; insofar as they introduce innovations and impose new conceptions, as the *Code Napoléon* did in areas of Western Germany, they emasculate the people's consciousness. The Historical School violently opposed any attempt at codification and rationalization of existing legal customs.

To what extent can these notions be connected with Hegel? In his *Philosophy of Right* Hegel stated that the *Volksgeist* endows the state with its unique chracter.[29] But beneath the identity of the term, there exists a difference of content and principles. For the Jurists, the *Volksgeist* is an essence creating law, morality, religion, and language. It is a mythical quality which takes on various forms and is implicit in the people, working hidden and unknown to all. But for Hegel the *Volksgeist* does not *create* the unique character of each people, but is the *product* of its concrete arrangements in the realms of religion, tradition, and the like.

The Hegelian *Volksgeist* is *identical* with the features it is describing, and does not *create* them, as the Jurists and the Romantics generally held. For them it is the unconscious creator of law, for Hegel the conscious product aware of itself.[30] The Hegelian concept is descriptive, while that of the Jurists is genetic.[d] Furthermore, Hegel's term is a rational one,

[d] In two respects the contrast between Hegel and the Jurists is not as clear as it might be. In the preceding three sentences the Hegelian *Volksgeist* is twice called the *product* of that with which in the central sentence it seems to be *identical,* and the author himself italicizes these words. He also says in the central sentence that it "does not *create* them"; but in the second sentence of the second paragraph of section V we are told that "each *Volksgeist* has to create a state."

Then, at the end of the present paragraph, the concept of the Jurists is said to be "naturalistic" and "positivist"; but up to this point it had seemed to be romantic and mystical, and in footnote 37 the author speaks of "the general romantic outlook." w.k.

while that of the Jurists is naturalistic, an *Ursache* of all social existence. Marcuse rightly observed[31] that the Jurists' conception is a positivist reaction to the rationalism immanent in the Hegelian *Volksgeist*.

The phenomenological similarity between law and language, as proposed by the Jurists, is also very remote from Hegel's view. For him, law embodies a rational, universalistic content, while language is an expression of chance attachment and arbitrary external affiliation. For Hegel the content of law embodies rational ethical qualities, while language is morally irrelevant: one legal norm may be said to be morally superior to another; it would be nonsense to say anything like this about languages.

Nor is this all: for Hegel the Idea, as an ethical quality realizing and embodying itself, attains realization only through its objectification in the world of phenomena, in its institutionalization. Where law is concerned this process of objectification of the ethical qualities takes place by explicit legislation and promulgation which posits the law as an objective fact, and not a mere subjective wish.[32]

From this derived Hegel's specific support for such works of codification as that of Justinian, Frederick the Great, and Napoleon.[33] On this issue Hegel specifically criticized the ideas of the Historical School and of Ludwig von Haller. He saw their opposition to an objective statute law as a shibboleth for their subjectivist, relativist, and irrational philosophical premises.[34] As the criterion for the existence of a traditional customary law is subjective (whether it is known or has already been forgotten), it is basically arbitrary and unclear. From this point of view Hegel argued against the anomalies of the unreformed English Common Law of the 1820s.[35]

Hegel was unable to accept the subjective test of law for an additional reason: it effaced the difference between law, which is objective, and personal morality, which is the specific province of subjectivity.[36] By maintaining a difference between the realms of law and private morality, Hegel also maintained the dual existence of state and society, amalgamated into one concept in the Jurists' theory and by the whole romantic movement.

Since Hegel's notions of law are rational categories of universal applicability, the positive content of the law cannot be derived from any national characteristics: the law is one and universal.[37] Hence his positive sympathy with the introduction of the rational Napoleonic Code, which swept away so much old dead wood and was viewed by Hegel as a step toward the victory of the universal general norms of law; after all, Hegel's *Philosophy of Right* is an abstraction of those norms, a blueprint for their inevitable institutionalization.

Hegel devoted one whole essay to a controversy concerning the validity of an actual customary traditional law, his long article on the constitutional struggle in Württemberg, in which he attacked the attitude of those who supported the validity of the traditional customary feudal law of that kingdom. Around the banner of the Good Old Law had gathered members of the Historical School of Law, the romantic supporters of the national folk-poet Uhland and the aristocratic circles of Württemberg, whose traditional rights stood to suffer from any rationalization and modernization of the legal system. In the same fierce language in which he had rejected the attempt to revive German tribal mythology, Hegel here rejected the attempt to uphold antiquated traditional law on the ground that it is the "primeval," "original," "old" law. For him, the very reliance on historical rights was utterly baseless, as it proved nothing:

> The question whether what is accepted as an acient law and an existing right is good or bad cannot be decided solely by the *age* of the legal arrangement concerned. The abolition of human sacrifice and of slavery, putting an end to feudal despotism, and the abolition of an infinite number of other iniquitous institutions, has been invariably the abolition of something which had been valid law in its time. It has been repeatedly stressed that rights do not disappear with time, and that a hundred years of iniquity cannot make injustice into justice.[38]

There exist, therefore, immanent rational criteria for the critique of social arrangements, and reliance on the past possesses no validating powers for the present. Such validation is possible only in the sphere of past events which always symbolize lower stages of consciousness. Whoever desires to remain within the confines of historical arrangements is reversing historical development, Hegel wrote in a passage in which he coupled social progress with a conscious effort at codification:

> The sun and the planets have their laws too, but they do not know them. Savages are governed by impulses, customs, and feelings, but they are unconscious of this. When right is posited as law and is known, every accident of feeling vanishes together with the form of revenge, sympathy and selfishness, and in this way the right attains for the first time its true determinacy and is given its due honour. [39]

These four characteristics of the Historical School are those that set them off from Hegel: legal positivism, seeing the *Volksgeist* as the unconscious original creator of law, aspiration to arrive at an original *Ur*-German law, and rejection of the value of conscious and explicit codification.

V

Only one aspect of Hegel's philosophy of history can be discussed here: the allegation that his philosophy of history is linked with German nationalism. To support the charge it is argued: first Hegel saw historical development in cycles of nations in successive order ruling over the entire world; and he saw the present age being realized among the German peoples, and as he conceived the present age to be the supreme stage of historical development, there is here correspondence with the Nazi idea of German supremacy.

Now, it is true that the formal division of the *Philosophy of History* into oriental, Greek, Roman, and Germanic periods points to the interpretation of epochs characterized each by a different dominant nation. But these stages, though characterized by successive *Volksgeister,* are not characterized by the political domination of any one national state: true, each *Volksgeist* has to create a state, but this is by no means *one, national* state. The Greek *polis, any* Greek *polis,* was the outcome of the Greek *Volksgeist,* although Greece never achieved political and national unification. Achieving a state means achieving self-consciousness: wherever there exists a body of people who see in some general political arrangements the embodiment of their essential will, there you have a state. How many states will be the outcome of any particular *Volksgeist* is immaterial: in the Greek case it was probably several hundred. Ethnic, linguistic, or racial frontiers have nothing to do with it. The Greek world was declining when it achieved its political unity by an outside agent and Meinecke saw this as a clear indication that Hegel never considered or valued or preached "national" unity.[40] He had nothing in common with later German historiography, already infected by nationalism, which criticized the Greeks, as Mommsen did, for not achieving unification. But the criticism was really aimed at contemporary Germany. The later German veneration for the Roman Empire cannot be found in Hegel, who had some rather harsh words to say about Roman imperialism, and who unqualifiedly preferred the Greek spirit to the Roman.[41]

But there is a frequently cited famous passage from the *Philosophy of History*, in which Hegel seemed to maintain that every World Historical Nation had an absolute right to dominance during its period of hegemony.[42] From this Popper and McGovern, to say nothing of general textbooks of history and political science, conclude that Hegel believed in world domination by one nation, Germany.

This interpretation, however, does not really sustain examination. It is mainly a projection of a twentieth-century situation back into Hegel's time and mind. Hegel never ascribed *political domination* to what he termed World Historical Nations. They seemed to possess quite different attributes: "All historical peoples embody power of literary creation, poetry, art, sculpture and painting, science and philosophy."[43] The *absolute right* is not in the realm of international politics, but in the sphere of cultural leadership. Thus, divided classical Greece was the stage at which the Greek spirit was dominant. Hegel was quite explicit that the Greek World never had any *political* meanings, that it was a cultural sphere—Magna Graecia.[44] The time of universal Greek political hegemony, during and after the Macedonian Empire, was, according to Hegel, a period of decadence.

Thus, it may be concluded that Hegel's cycles of history are cycles of the cultural sphere, and not of political domination or military conquest, and this may also explain the meaning of what Hegel termed the Germanic World or period.

Initially, some semantic misunderstanding has to be cleared. Hegel termed the last phase of historical development *die germanische Welt* (the Germanic World) and not *die deutsche Welt* (the German World). It is significant—and deplorable—that Sibree in his translation of the *Philosophy of History* never distinguished between *germanisch* and *deutsch* and translated both terms as "German."[45] The term "Germanic" is, in the German usage, always used to connote a cultural sphere, and had no political implications, whereas the term "German" aroused in Anglo-Saxon readers of the last half century every possible association with German political world domination.

Hegel, in generally referring to this Germanic period as the *Christian World,* may have revealed his real meaning: the last and present historical epoch has nothing to do with German political domination, which would be completely incompatible with Hegel's own opposition to German unification. Like the former historical periods, this period has to be interpreted in cultural terms, and the only meaning behind the term "Germanic World" in Hegel implies that Hegel saw in Western Civilization the highlight of mankind's spiritual development. The values of this Germanic world are Christian values; in spite of the fact that his new and last historical phase started with the disintegration of the Roman world, Hegel never forgot that the bearers of the new civilization, the Germanic tribes, accepted the Christianity of the Roman culture. The principle dominating Europe, though sometimes called Germanic by

Hegel, is the Christian principle, and not an original Germanic contribution to World History: no *Ur-Volk* mythology can be ascribed to Hegel's terming the last phase as a Germanic one, for he explicitly wrote:

> It is extremely important to stress how different is the course of Germanic history from that of the Greeks and Romans. While the latter embodied their own original principles, the impulse to Germanic development was imparted to the Germanics by alien culture. The principles realized by them, their culture and development, their law and religion, were borrowed.[46]

There could be no stronger condemnation of the Germanistic interpretation of history than this: while Herder and the Romantics were basing their national ideology on the "originality" (*Ursprünglichkeit*) of the Germanics, Hegel regarded them as the bearers of a foreign culture and saw in this their main virtue, as their own "original" culture could never have attained any historical importance because of its inherent barbarism:

> Before the Germanics adopted the Christian principles, they had lived in a state of barbarism. Their pagan religion was superficial and lacking essential contents. . . . Germanic law is not true law, for under it murder is not a crime from the point of view of moral values, but merely a private offense compensated by a payment of damages. . . . The Germanic individual is free, but free as the wild animal is free, possessing no value as a moral being. . . . Ever since Tacitus, much has been said of the ancient original liberty of the Germanics. But woe to us were we to confuse this state of savagery and barbarism with a state of liberty, and let us not be induced to follow Rousseau's fallacy, who saw in the wild American Indians the embodiment of liberty.[47]

The Germanic world is not, therefore, an ethnic, racial, or political nation. It is Christian Europe, Western Civilization, including according to Hegel, not only Germany, but Spain and France, England and Italy as well—and, perhaps, even Russia.[48] It is not associated with the geographical region inhabited by Germanic Tribes, just as it has no connection with the modern political hegemony of Germany. From a political point of view the settlement of 1815, basically antinational, corresponded to the Christian and conservative *Weltanschauung* of Hegel. This *gens Christiana* had no need for the subjectivist nationalist consciousness or for the ethnic-linguistic links, which are accidental and have no rational or moral meaning. Hegel envisaged the modern world as a world containing a multiplicity of political units and powers, in the manner of classical Greece.[49] It is held together not by political power, but by what Hegel metaphysically termed the Spirit, realizing in Christian Europe, what Hegel understood, with a strong Lutheran undercurrent, as liberty: the recognition of necessity.

One may beg to differ from this sort of metaphysics, and historically Hegel's analysis seems to be rather naive, though, for a generation torn by a quarter century of wars, this may be understandable. This comes out clearly when one observes that according to Hegel the unifying common spirit was also affecting a humanization of international conduct in his contemporary world: "The European peoples form a family in accordance with the universal principle underlying their legal codes, their customs, and their civilization. This principle has accordingly modified their international conduct in a state of affairs (i.e., war), otherwise dominated by the mutual infliction of evil."[50]

To read here a nationalist meaning twists Hegel's philosophy into meaninglessness. It is understandable how such a peculiar misreading gained currency in a generation which projected its own image of German unity, German nationalism, and finally Nazism upon the entire German philosophy and history of the nineteenth century. The annals of the historiography of Hegel's teaching, to which some allusions were made at the outset of this discussion, are themselves an interesting chapter in the metamorphosis of the modern *Zeitgeist*. But this explanation cannot alter the nature of Hegel's philosophy itself.

One reservation should, perhaps, be made. The development of modern nationalism may be attributed to two main currents: on the one hand, the increased value attributed to the cultural and ethnic association and to romantic communal togetherness; on the other hand, it sprang up from the crystallization of the modern territorial state that constituted the context in which the national claims were realized.

Both are distinct phenomena, caused by different historical and cultural developments. They met in the course of the nineteenth century through the grafting of the national *idea* into the political *structure* of the territorial machinery produced by monarchical absolutism.

The first phenomenon was completely alien to Hegel. But in relation to the second, more "political," or even better, *étatist* aspect, Hegel's thought may stand in some contributory relation. As A.D. Lindsay once remarked, [51] the transition from the dynastic to the national state arose out of the transition from the individual's allegiance first to his ruler, and later to his fellow citizens in the political unit, the mediation for such allegiance being furnished by rational, political, and universalistic-anonymous institutions. Political obligation, so to speak, was refined and institutionalized. To this development Hegel's contribution was undoubtedly large, for in his philosophy the political sphere became the dominant set of interhuman relations. The political sphere, by becoming dominant, makes the modern state strong in comparison with other historical political arrangements, and, though it was not Hegel's intention, this powerful state became an instrument of nationalism—for without a clear-cut idea of a modern, strong and rationally-organized state, nationalism could not have laid its claim to primacy.

In *this*, then, may lie Hegel's contribution, albeit an unconscious one, to the crystallization of the modern national state. It is, perhaps, dialectically fascinating to discover that the doctrine of a thinker who rejected any manifestation of nationalism, should be found to have ultimately contributed to this process from an unexpected angle. But, to Hegel, familiar as he was with the "cunning of reason" (*List der Vernunft*), possibly this would not have been surprising.

NOTES

1. This is an extended version of a paper read before the Israel Historical Association in Jerusalem. I am deeply indebted for the help I was privileged to receive from Professor J. L. Talmon, under whom this study was conducted. I am further indebted to Professor Karl Popper of the London School of Economics, Dr. J. Rodman of Harvard University, Dr. Z. A. Pelczynski of Pembroke College, Oxford, and Mr. R. Friedman of Johns Hopkins for the stimulating discussions I had with them. That we sometimes had to agree to differ did not diminish the value of those discussions in clarifying my own ideas.

2. *Briefe von und an Hegel*, ed. J. Hoffmeister (Hamburg, 1952), I, 120.

3. *Ibid.*, I, 137. [*der Geist über geistlosen Verstand* might be rendered more literally as "spirit over spiritless understanding." w.k.]

4. *Ibid.*, II, 6.

5. *Ibid.*, II, 27.

6. *Ibid.*, II, 14–15.

7. *Ibid.*, II, 23.

8. *Hegels Schriften zur Politik und Rechtsphilosophie*, ed. G. Lasson (Leipzig, 1913), p. 159.

9. G.W.F. Hegel, *Vorlesungern über die Philosophie der Weltgeschichte*, ed. G. Lasson (Leipzig, 1920), p. 937 (subsequently referred to as *Weltgeschichte*).

10. *Hegel's Philosophy of Right*, trans. T. M. Knox (Oxford, 1945), § 322.

11. *Ibid.*, § 209; cf. also § 270. See Avineri, "The Hegelian Position on the Emancipation of the Jews," *Iyyun* (Jersusalem, 1960), XXV, No. 2, 134–136 (in Hebrew).

12. G. W. F. Hegel, *Die Vernunft in der Geschichte—Einleitung zur Geschichtsphilosophie*, ed. J. Hoffmeister (Hamburg, 1955), p. 159 (subsequently referred to as *Einleitung*).

13. K. R. Popper, *The Open Society and Its Enemies* (Princeton, 1950), pp. 255–273.

14. H. Heller, *Hegel und der nationale Machtstaatsgedanke in Deutschland* (Leipzig & Berlin, 1921).

15. E. F. Carritt, "Hegel and Prussianism," *Philosophy*, XV (Jan. 1940), 51–56; J. Bowle, *Politics and Opinion in the 19th Century* (London, 1954), pp. 34–50; W. M. McGovern, *From Luther to Hitler* (New York, 1940), pp. 317–355. Cf. also the recent work by A. Hacker, *Political Theory: Philosophy, Ideology, Science* (New York, 1961), pp. 438–445. This view, however, is by no means unchallenged. Cf. Georg Lukacs, "Der deutsche Faschismus und Hegel," in his *Schicksalswende: Beiträge zu einer neuen deutschen Ideologie* (Berlin, 1948), pp. 37–67; H. Marcuse, *Reason and Revolution,* 2nd ed. (London, 1955); W. Kaufmann, *From Shakespeare to Existentialism* (New York, 1960); also F. Meinecke, *Weltbürgertum und Nationalstaat,* 3, Aufl. (Munich and Berlin, 1915), pp. 275ff.

16. R. Haym, *Hegel und seine Zeit* (Berlin, 1857).

17. H. V. Treitschke, *Politics,* trans. B. Dugdale and T. de Bille (London, 1916), I, 22–23, 53.

18. K. Köstlin, *Hegel in philosophischer, politischer und nationaler Beziehung* (Tübingen, 1870), pp. 158–165, 174.

19. *Hegels Schriften zur Politik und Rechtsphilosophie*, pp. 24–25.

20. G. W. F. Hegel, *On Christianity: Early Theological Writings,* trans. T. M. Knox and R. Kroner (New York, 1961), p. 69.

21. *Ibid.*, p. 77.

22. *Ibid.*, p. 152.
23. *Ibid.*, pp. 158–159.
24. *Ibid.*, p. 146.
25. *Ibid.*, p. 149.
26. Quoted by Köstlin, *op. cit.*, p. 170 (my italics).
27. For the connection between the Historical School and political romanticism and nationalism, cf. C. Schmitt, *Politische Romantik*, 2. Aufl. (Munich, 1925), pp. 46ff. For the indebtedness of the Nazi lawyers to this tradition, see O. Dietrich, *Die philosophischen Grundlagen des Nationalsozialismus* (Breslau, 1935); H. Nicolai, *Die rassengesetzliche Rechtslehre* (Munich, 1933).
28. G. Rexius, "Studien zur Staatslehre der historischen Schule," *Historische Zeitschrift*, Vol. 107 (1911), 520; H. V. Kantorowicz, "Volksgeist und historische Schule," *ibid.*, Vol. 108 (1912), 303ff; S. Brie, *Der Volksgeist bei Hegel und in der historischen Rechtsschule* (Berlin and Leipzig, 1909), pp. 25ff.
29. §§ 33, 331, addition to 259.
30. Cf. J. Löwenstein, *Hegels Staatsidee—Ihr Doppelgesicht und Einfluss im 19. Jahrhundert* (Berlin, 1927), pp. 41–42.
31. *Reason and Revolution,* p. 237.
32. *Philosophy of Right,* §§ 349–350.
33. *Ibid.*, § 211.
34. *Ibid.*, Introduction, p. 10; §§ 258–259.
35. *Ibid.*, § 211. The unreformed English Common Law is frequently used by Hegel as an example of the anxiety, irrationality and eventual cruelty of uncodified customary law. He kept a whole collection of press-cuttings illustrating some of the more blatant absurdities of early nineteenth-century Common Law. These cuttings have been published in *Hegels Berliner Schriften*, ed. J. Hoffmeister (Hamburg, 1956), sec. VIII, ch. 31, pp. 718–724.
36. *Philosophy of Right,* § 213. Hegel's disciple, Edward Gans, held the same position in his Introduction to his master's *Philosophy of Right*, pp. xiii–xiv, as well as in his own work, *Erbrecht in weltgeschichtlicher Entwicklung* (Berlin, 1824), I, vi.
37. This has been characteristically criticized as being contradictory to Hegel's system by Ferdinand Lassalle, *System der erworbenen Rechte*, 2. Aufl., I, xv–xvii, 58–61. Lassalle, in spite of his Hegelianism, was very much influenced by the Historical School (his book was dedicated to one of its leading members), and his concept of *Volksgeist* is identical with their and with the general romantic outlook. Those interested in the involved problem of Lassalle's nationalism may find this of some interest.
38. *Hegels Schriften zur Politik und Rechtsphilosophie*, p. 199. That this attitude is very far from a Burkean one should be borne in mind, especially by those who tend to see in Hegel strong traces of Burke's influence. The fact that Hegel accepted rational criteria for a critique of social conditions should make his attitude quite distinct from Burke's, in spite of the fact that Hegel did not go very far in applying those criteria to immediate reality.
39. *Philosophy of Right,* addition to § 211.
40. *Op. cit.*, p. 275. Cf. also F. Rosenzweig, *Hegel und der Staat* (Berlin, 1920), II, 5.
41. *Einleitung*, p. 250; *Weltgeschichte*, pp. 705, 711.
42. *Philosophy of Right,* § 347. [*History* in the sentence above is clearly a slip. W.K.]

43. *Einleitung,* p. 174.
44. *Weltgeschichte,* pp. 533–542.
45. *Hegel's Philosophy of History,* trans. J. Sibree, new edition (New York, 1956), pp. xv, 341. I have refrained from using this translation, and rendered my own translation of the passages quoted from the various parts of the *Philosophy of History,* because of the rather unreliable and fragmentary German edition which served as a basis for Sibree's translation. See Hoffmeister's Appendix to his edition of the *Einleitung* for a detailed account of these problems.
46. *Weltgeschichte,* p. 758.
47. *Ibid.,* p. 775.
48. *Ibid.,* pp. 774ff.
49. *Ibid.,* p. 761.
50. *Philosophy of Right,* addition to § 339. A similar note is voiced by Hegel in his *Aesthetics:* "In contemporary Europe, every nation is limited by another one, and cannot, therefore, embark on a course of war against another European nation" (*Werke,* ed. Glockner, XIV, 335). Cf. *Weltgeschichte* p. 761 and Avineri, "The Problem of War in Hegel's Thought," *Journal of the History of Ideas,* XXII (1961), 463–474.
51. *The Modern Democratic State* (London, 1943), I, 146–149.

10 The Hegel Myth and Its Method

WALTER KAUFMANN

1. HEGEL'S IMPORTANCE

Hegel was not a pagan like Shakespeare and Goethe but a philosopher who considered himself Christian and tried to do from a Protestant point of view what Aquinas had attempted six hundred years earlier: he sought to fashion a synthesis of Greek philosophy and Christianity, making full use of the labors of his predecessors. Among these he counted not only the great philosophers from Heraclitus and Plato down to Kant, Fichte, and Schelling but also such world-

The first version of this paper appeared in *The Philosophical Review,* October 1951. The revised version here reprinted was included in Kaufmann's book, *From Shakespeare to Existentialism* (Boston, Beacon Press, 1959), published in England under the title *The Owl and the Nightingale* (London, Faber and Faber, 1960). The Doubleday Anchor Books paperback edition is subtitled "A New Edition, with Additions," but the present essay was not revised further. It should be noted that this paper antedates Chapters 5–9 above.

historic individuals as Paul and the men who had made the French Revolution. As he saw it, philosophy did not stand between religion and poetry but above both. Philosophy was, according to him, its age comprehended in thought, and—to exaggerate a little—the philosopher's task was to *comprehend* what the religious person and the poet *feel*.

Hegel's enormous importance becomes clear as soon as we reflect on his historic role. There is, *first,* his direct influence, which appears not only in philosophic idealism, which, at the turn of the last century, dominated British and American philosophy—Bradley, Bosanquet, McTaggart, T. H. Green, and Royce, to give but five examples—but also in almost all subsequent histories of philosophy, beginning with the epoch-making works of Erdmann, Zeller, and Kuno Fischer. It was Hegel who established the history of philosophy as a central academic discipline and as part of the core of any philosophic education. It was also Hegel who established the view that the different philosophic systems that we find in history are to be comprehended in terms of development and that they are generally one-sided because they owe their origins to a reaction against what has gone before.

Secondly, most of the more important philosophic movements since his death have been so many reactions against Hegel's own idealism and cannot be fully understood without some grasp of his philosophy. The first two great revolts were those of Kierkegaard and Marx, who swallowed easily as much of his philosophy as they rejected: notably, his dialectic. Today Marx's dialectic dominates a large part of the total population of the globe, while Kierkegaard's has been adapted by some of the most outstanding thinkers of the free world, notably Heidegger and Tillich, Barth and Niebuhr.

Two later revolts against Hegelianism dominate English and American philosophy in the twentieth century: pragmatism and analytic philosophy. William James, though occasionally he attacked Hegel himself, reconstructed Hegel somewhat in the image of his Harvard colleague, Royce, who was then the outstanding American idealist; while Moore, at Cambridge, who was joined by Russell, led the fight against the influence of Bradley and McTaggart.

One of the few things on which the analysts, pragmatists, and existentialists agree with the dialectical theologians is that Hegel is to be repudiated: their attitude toward Kant, Aristotle, Plato, and the other great philosophers is not at all unanimous even within each movement; but opposition to Hegel is part of the platform of all four, and of the Marxists, too. Oddly, the man whom all these movements take to be so crucially important is but little known to most of their adherents; very few indeed have read as many as two of the four books that Hegel published.

Hegel is known largely through secondary sources and a few incriminating slogans and generalizations. The resulting myth, however, lacked a comprehensive, documented statement till Karl Popper found a place for it in his widely discussed book, *The Open Society and Its Enemies.* After it had gone through three impressions in England, a revised one-volume edition was brought out in the United States in 1950, five years after its original appearance.

2. CRITIQUE OF A CRITIC

To explode the popular Hegel legend one can hardly do better than to deal in some detail with Popper's Hegel chapter. This involves a temporary departure from religion and poetry, but the development "from Shakespeare to existentialism" cannot be understood without some grasp of Hegel and some discussion of the widely accepted image of Hegel. Moreover, Hegel is so frequently mentioned in contemporary discussions that it is intrinsically worth while to show how wrong many widespread assumptions about him are. Thirdly, our study should include some explicit consideration of questions of method, and especially of common pitfalls. Finally, we shall have occasion, as we develop Hegel's actual views, to call attention to the religious roots of some of his most characteristic notions. . . . Gross falsifications of history are not the monopoly of Miniver Cheevy. Forward-looking liberals and even believers in "piecemeal social engineering," like Popper, often distort history, too. And so, alas, did Hegel.

A detailed critique of Popper's sixty-nine pages on Hegel may be prefaced with a motto from Nietzsche's *Ecce Homo:* "I only avail myself of the person as of a strong magnifying glass with which one can render visible a general but creeping calamity which it is otherwise hard to get hold of."

The calamity in our case is twofold. First, Popper's treatment contains more misconceptions about Hegel than any other single essay. Secondly, if one agrees with Popper that "intellectual honesty is fundamental for everything we cherish" (p. 253), one should protest against his methods; for although his hatred of totalitarianism is the inspiration and central motif of his book, his methods are unfortunately similar to those of totalitarian "scholars"—and they are spreading in the free world, too.

3. SCHOLARSHIP

Although the mere presense of nineteen pages of notes suggests that his attack on Hegel is based on careful scholarship, Popper ignores the most important works on his subject. This is doubly serious because he is intent on psychologizing the men he attacks: he deals not only with their arguments but also—if not altogether more—with their alleged motives. This practice is as dangerous as it is fashionable, but in some cases there is no outright evidence to the contrary: one can only say that Popper credits all the men he criticizes, except Marx, with the worst possible intentions. (Marx he credits with the best intentions.)

In the case of Hegel, there is voluminous evidence that Popper ignores: beginning with Dilthey's pioneering study of 1906 and the subsequent publication of Hegel's early writings, ample material has been made available concerning the development of his ideas. There is even a two-volume study by Franz Rosenzweig, the friend of Martin Buber, that specifically treats the development of those ideas with which Popper is concerned above all: *Hegel und der Staat.*

Furthermore, Popper has relied largely on *Scribner's Hegel Selections,* a little anthology for students that contain not a single complete work. Like Gilson in *The Unity of Philosophical Experience* (p. 246), Popper takes over such a gross mistranslation as "the State is the march of God through the world," although the original says merely that it is the way of God with the world that there should be the State, and even this sentence is lacking in the text published by Hegel and comes from one of the editor's additions to the posthumous edition of *The Philosophy of Right*—and the editor admitted in his Preface that, though these additions were based on lecture notes, "the choice of words" was sometimes his rather than Hegel's.

Popper also appears to be unaware of crucial passages, if not entire works, that are not included in these *Selections;* for example, the passage on war in Hegel's first book, which shows that his later conception of war, which is far more moderate, was not adopted to accomodate the king of Prussia, as Popper maintains. The passage on war in Hegel's *Phenomenology of the Spirit,* in the section on "The Ethical World," was written when Hegel—a Swabian, not a Prussian—admired Napoleon and was published in 1807, a year after Prussia's devastating defeat at Jena. Hegel's views on war will be considered soon (in section 11); but questions of method require our attention first.

4. QUILT QUOTATIONS

This device, used by other writers, too, has not received the criticism it deserves. Sentences are picked from various contexts, often even out of different books, enclosed by a single set of quotation marks, and separated only by three dots, which are generally taken to indicate no more than the omission of a few words. Plainly, this device can be used to impute to an author views he never held.

Here, for example, is a quilt quotation about war and arson: "Do not think that I have come to bring peace on earth; I have not come to bring peace, but a sword. . . . I came to cast fire upon the earth. . . . Do you think that I have come to give peace on earth? No, I tell you. . . . Let him who has no sword sell his mantle and buy one." This is scarcely the best way to establish Jesus' views of war and arson. In the works of some philosophers, too—notably, Nietzsche—only the context can show whether a word is meant literally.

The writings of Hegel and Plato abound in admittedly one-sided statements that are clearly meant to formulate points of view that are then shown to be inadequate and are countered by another perspective. Thus an impressive quilt quotation could be patched together to convince gullible readers that Hegel was—depending on the "scholar's" plans—either emphatically for or utterly opposed to, say, "equality." But the understanding of Hegel would be advanced ever so much more by citing one of his remarks about equality *in context,* showing how it is a step in an argument that is designed to lead the reader to a better comprehension of equality and not to enlist his emotions either for it or against it.

Even those who would not reduce all philosophy to such analyses should surely grant the ambiguity of words like equality and freedom, good and God—and also that philosophers can be of service by distinguishing some of the different meanings of such terms instead of aping politicians by assuring us that they are heartily in favor of all four. Popper writes like a district attorney who wants to persuade his audience that Hegel was against God, freedom, and equality—and uses quilt quotations to convince us.

The first of these (p. 227) consists of eight fragments of which every single one is due to one of Hegel's students and was not published by him. Although Popper scrupulously marks references to Gans's additions to the *Philosophy of*

Right with an "L" and invariably gives all the references for his quilt quotations—e.g., "For the eight quotations in this paragraph, cf. *Selections* . . ."—a few readers indeed will recall when they come to the Notes at the end of the book that "the eight quotations" are the quilt quotations that they took for a single passage. And Popper advises his readers "first to read without interruption through the text of a chapter, and then to turn to the Notes."

Quilt quotations invite comparison with composite photographs. In a campaign for a seat in the U. S. Senate, one such photograph was used that showed one candidate shaking hands with the head of the Communist party. It matters little whether it was labeled in fine print "composite photograph."

To be sure, quotations and photographs that are not patched together may be grossly unfair. But a self-respecting candidate will not use patched-up photographs of his opponent; and a scholar should not use a quilt quotation to indict the men he criticizes.

5. "INFLUENCE"

No conception is bandied about more unscrupulously in the history of ideas than "influence." Popper's notion of it is so utterly unscientific that one should never guess that he has done important work on logic and on scientific method. At best, it is reducible to *post hoc, ergo propter hoc.* Thus he speaks of "the Hegelian Bergson" (p. 256 and n. 66) and assumes, without giving any evidence whatever, that Bergson, Smuts, Alexander, and Whitehead were all interested in Hegel, simply because they were "evolutionists" (p. 225 and n. 6).

What especially concerns Popper—and many another critic of German thinkers—is the "influence" that the accused had on the Nazis. His Hegel chapter is studded with quotations from recent German writers, almost all of which are taken from *The War Against the West* by Kolnai. In this remarkable book Friedrich Gundolf, Werner Jaeger (Harvard), and Max

Scheler are pictured as "representative of Nazism or at least its general trend and atmosphere." Kolnai is also under the impression that the men who contributed most "to the rise of National Socialism as a creed" were Nietzsche "and Stefan George, less great but, perhaps because of his homosexuality, more directly instrumental in creating the Third Reich" (p. 14); that Nietzsche was a "half-Pole" (p. 453); that the great racist H. S. Chamberlain "was a mellow Englishman tainted by noxious German influences" (p. 455); and that Jaspers is a "follower" of Heidegger (p. 207). It would seem advisable to check the context of any quotations from Kolnai's book before one uses them, but Kolnai generally gives no references. Popper writes:

> I am greatly indebted to Kolnai's book, which has made it possible for me to quote in the remaining part of this chapter a considerable number of authors who would otherwise have been inaccessible to me. (I have not, however, always followed the wording of Kolnai's translations.)

He evidently changed the wording without checking the originals or even the context.

Popper uses quotation after quotation from Kolnai to point out supposed similarities with Hegel, but never stops to ask whether the men he cites had read Hegel, what they thought of him, or where, in fact, they did get their ideas. Thus we are told that the idea of "fame is revived by Hegel" (p. 266), for Hegel spoke of fame as a "reward" of the men whose deeds are recorded in our history books—which would seem a trite enough idea that could also be ascribed to scores of sincere democrats—but Popper goes on: "and Stapel, a propagator of the new paganized Christianity, promptly [i.e., one hundred years later] repeats [*sic*]: 'All great deeds were done for the sake of fame or glory.' " This is surely quite a different idea and not trite but false. Popper himself admits that Stapel "is even more radical than Hegel." Surely, one must question the relevance of the whole section dealing with Stapel and other recent writers; this is not history of ideas but an attempt to establish guilt by association on the same page—in the hope, it seems, that *semper aliquid haeret.*

It is also the height of naiveté. A quick dip into a good dictionary of quotations would have shown Popper a great many closer parallels to Stapel than he found in Hegel. Perhaps the most extreme, and also the most memorable, formulations are found in some poets whose influence would be hard to gauge. Shakespeare writes:

> *Let fame, that all hunt after in their lives,*
> *Live register'd upon our brazen tombs.*

And though these lines occur in one of his comedies, *Love's Labour's Lost,* he certainly did not think meanly of fame. Ben Jonson even went a step further in *Sejanus* (I, ii): "Contempt of fame begets contempt of virtue." And Friedrich Schiller voiced a still more radical view—in a poem that many German school children learn by heart, *Das Siegesfest,* which deals with the Greeks' celebration of their triumph over Troy:

> *Of the goods that man has cherished*
> *Not one is as high as fame;*
> *When the body has long perished*
> *What survives is the great name.*

For every Nazi who knew Hegel's remarks about fame there must have been dozens who knew these lines. Does that prove Schiller a bad man? Or does it show that he was responsible for Nazism?

Besides, Popper often lacks the knowledge of who influenced whom. Thus he speaks of Heidegger and "his master Hegel" (p. 271) and asserts falsely that Jaspers began as a follower "of the essentialist philosophers Husserl and Scheler" (p. 270). More important, he contrasts the vicious Hegel with superior men "such as Schopenhauer or J. F. Fries" (p. 223), and he constantly makes common cause with Schopenhauer against the allegedly protofascist Hegel, whom he blames even for the Nazis' racism—evidently unaware that Fries and Schopenhauer, unlike the mature Hegel, *were* anti-Semites.

Hegel's earliest essays, which he himself did not publish, show that he started out with violent prejudices against the Jews. These essays will be considered later; but they are not represented in *Scribner's Hegel Selections* and hence were not exploited by Popper. Nor have they exerted any perceivable influence. When Hegel later became a man of influence, he insisted that the Jews should be granted equal rights because civic rights belong to man because he is a man and not on account of his ethnic origins or his religion.

Fries, who was Hegel's predecessor at the University of Heidelberg, has often been considered a great liberal, and Hegel has often been condemned for taking a strong stand against him; it is rarely, if ever, mentioned in this context that Fries published a pamphlet in the summer of 1816 in which he called for the "extermination" of Jewry. It appeared simultaneously as a review article in *Heidelbergische Jahrbücher der Litteratur* and as a pamphlet with the title "How the Jews endanger the prosperity and the character of the Germans." According to Fries, the Jews "were and are the bloodsuckers of the people" (p. 243) and "do not at all live and teach according to Mosaic doctrine but according to the Talmud" (p. 251) of which Fries conjures up a frightening picture. "Thus the Jewish caste . . . *should be exterminated completely* [*mit Stumpf und Stiel ausgerottet*] *because it is obviously of all secret and political societies and states within the state the most dangerous*" (p. 256). "Any immigration of Jews should be forbidden, their emigration should be promoted. Their freedom to marry should . . . be limited. . . . It should be forbidden that any Christian be hired by a Jew" (p. 260); and one should again force on them "a special mark on their clothing" (p. 261). In between, Fries protests: "Not against *the Jews,* our brothers, but against *Jewry* [*der Judenschaft*] we declare war" (p. 248).

This may help us to understand why Hegel, in the Preface to his *Philosophy of Right,* scorned Fries's substitution of "the pap of 'heart, friendship, and enthusiasm'" for moral laws. It would certainly have been unwise of the Jews to rely on Fries's brotherly enthusiasm.

Hegel's often obscure style may have evened the way for later obscurantism, but Fries's and Schopenhauer's flamboyant irrationalism was, stylistically, too, much closer to most Nazi literature. It does not follow that Fries influenced the Nazis. He was soon forgotten, till, in the twentieth century, Leonard Nelson, a Jewish philosopher, founded a neo-Friesian school that had nothing to do with Fries's racial prejudices. The one influential thinker whom Nelson succeeded in leading back to Fries was Rudolf Otto, the Protestant theologian, who is best known for his book on *The Idea of the Holy*. What makes that book so notable is its fine description of the "numinous" experience; but the confused discussion of "The Holy as an A Priori Category" and the romantic notions about "divining" are indebted to Fries.

Popper, though he has written an important book on *Die Logik der Forschung,* "The Logic of Research," does not find it necessary to check his hunches by research when he is concerned with influences in his Hegel chapter. He simply decrees that Hegel "represents the 'missing link,' as it were, between Plato and the modern form of totalitarianism. Most of the modern totalitarians are quite unaware that their ideas can be traced back to Plato. But many know of their indebtedness to Hegel" (p. 226). Seeing that the context indicates a reference to the Nazis and that all the totalitarians cited in this chapter are Fascists, not Communists, Popper only shows his ignorance of this brand of totalitarianism.

Hegel was rarely cited in the Nazi literature, and, when he was referred to, it was usually by way of disapproval. The Nazis' official "philosopher," Alfred Rosenberg, mentioned, and denounced, Hegel twice in his best-selling *Der Mythus des Zwanzigsten Jahrhunderts.* Originally published in 1930, this book had reached an edition of 878,000 copies by 1940. In the same book, a whole chapter is devoted to Popper's beloved Schopenhauer, whom Rosenberg admired greatly. Rosenberg also celebrates Plato as "one who wanted in the end to save his people [*Volk*] on a racial basis, through a forcible constitution, dictatorial in every detail." Rosenberg also stressed, and excoriated, the "Socratic" elements in Plato.

Plato, unlike Hegel, was widely read in German schools, and special editions were prepared for Greek classes in the *Gymnasium,* gathering together allegedly fascist passages. In his introduction to one such selection from the *Republic,* published by Teubner in the series of *Eclogae Graecolatinae,* Dr. Holtorf helpfully listed some of his relevant articles on Plato, including one in the *Völkischer Beobachter,* which was Hitler's own paper. Instead of compiling a list of the many similar contributions to the Plato literature, it may suffice to mention that Dr. Hans F. K. Günther, from whom the Nazis admittedly received their racial theories, also devoted a whole book to Plato—not to Hegel—as early as 1928. In 1935, a second edition was published.

Whether Hegel did, or did not, influence the Nazis may not be particularly relevant to Popper's central theses in his book— but then most of his book is not. His often stimulating ideas are amalgamated with a great deal of thoroughly unsound intellectual history; and Section V of his Hegel chapter (eighteen pages) is representative of the latter. It is also representative of scores of similar attempts by authors who have less to offer than Karl Popper.

6. VITUPERATION AND ALLEGATION OF MOTIVES

Although Popper, in his introduction, speaks of "the application of the critical and rational methods of science to the problems of the open society" (p. 3), he writes about Hegel in the accents of a prosecutor who addresses a jury. He says of Fichte and Hegel, "such clowns are taken seriously" (p. 249); he demands, "I ask whether it is possible to outdo this despicable perversion of everything that is decent" (p. 244); and he denounces "Hegel's hysterical historicism" (p. 253; cf. p. 269).

Hegel certainly has grievous faults. Among these is his obscure style, but it is dry and unemotional in the extreme. A detailed account of his almost incredibly unemotional style as a lecturer has been given by one of his students, H. G. Hotho, and is quoted in Hermann Glockner's *Hegel* (I, 440 ff.), and in Kuno Fisher's *Hegel,* too. If "hysterical" means, as Webster says, "wildly emotional," Popper deserves this epithet much more than Hegel. For all of Hegel's shortcomings, it seems wildly emotional indeed to say that "he is supreme only in his outstanding lack of originality" and was not even "talented" (p. 227). And "the critical and rational methods of science" could hardly establish Popper's contention that the philosophy of Jaspers is a "gangster" philosophy (p. 272). Nor is this proved by a note on "the gangster philosophy" in the back of the volume, which turns out to furnish us with a quilt quotation (see above) from Ernst von Solomon's book, *The Outlaws,* which bears no perceivable relation to Karl Jaspers—not to speak of Hegel.

Popper's allegation of motives is scarcely distinguishable from vituperation. Hegel is accused of "a perversion . . . of a sincere belief in God" (p. 244), but no evidence whatever is given to substantiate this charge. "Hegel's radical collectivism . . . depends on Frederick William III, king of Prussia" and his "one aim" was "to serve his employer, Frederick William of Prussia" (pp. 227 f.); and it is hinted that Hegel misused philosophy as a means of financial gain (p. 241); but Popper ignores the literature on this question, which includes, in addition to the volumes cited above, T. M. Knox's article on "Hegel and Prussianism" in *Philosophy,* January 1940, and his discussion with Carritt in the April and July issues.

Hegel, we are told, "wants to stop rational argument, and with it, scientific and intellectual progress" (p. 235), and his dialectics "are very largely designed to pervert the ideas of 1789" (p. 237). When Hegel explicitly comes out in favor of the things that, according to his accuser, he opposed, this is called "lip service" (ns. 11 and 43). Thus Popper claims—like Bäumler in his Nazi version of Nietzsche—that the man whom he professes to interpret did not mean what he clearly said. Quilt quotations are used to establish a man's views, and his explicit statements are discounted when they are inconvenient.

In the name of "the critical and rational methods of science," one must also protest against such emotional *ad hominem* arguments as that Heidegger's philosophy must be wrong because he became a Nazi later on (p. 271), or that "Haeckel can hardly be taken seriously as a philosopher or scientist. He called himself a free thinker, but this thinking was not sufficiently independent to prevent him from demanding in 1914 'the following fruits of victory . . .' " (n. 65). By the same token, one might seek to discredit Popper's philosophy of science by pointing to his treatment of Hegel, or Newton's physics by calling attention to his absorbing concern with magic, which Lord Keynes has described in his *Essays and Sketches in Biography.*

Popper's occasional references to "the doctrine of the chosen people," which he associates with totalitarianism, show little knowledge of the prophets though a great deal of emotion, and his references to Christianity are also based on sentiment rather than the logic of research. He is "for" Christianity, but means by it something that is utterly at variance with the explicit teachings of Paul, the Catholic Church, Luther, and Calvin.

Hegel's rejection of the adequacy of conscience as a guide in moral questions is countered by Popper's parenthesis, "that is to say, the moralists who refer, for example, to the New Testament" (p. 262)—as if no crimes had ever been committed in the name of the New Testament. Julius Streicher, in his violently anti-Semitic paper, *Der Stürmer,* constantly quoted the Gospel according to St. John.

One of the most important criticisms of Popper's approach, and of the large literature that resembles his attack on Hegel, might be summed up by citing Maritain's epigram from *Scholasticism and Politics* (p. 147): "If books were judged by the bad uses man can put them to, what book has been more misused than the Bible?"

7. HEGEL'S METAPHYSICS

Two simple points may illustrate how thoroughly Popper misunderstands the whole framework of Hegel's thought. First, he claims that Hegel taught that "self-evidence is the same as truth" (p. 237), although Hegel's first book begins with the denial of this view and Hegel never changed his mind about this.

The second point is more important because Hegel has so often been misunderstood in this way. "Hegel believes, with Aristotle, that the Ideas or essences are *in* the things in flux; or more precisely (as far as we can treat a Hegel with precision), Hegel teaches that they are identical with the things in flux: "Everything actual is an Idea,' he says" (p. 231). Yet one need not look farther than Royce's helpful article on Hegel's terminology in Baldwin's *Dictionary of Philosophy and Psychology* to find that "actual" is, in Hegel's work, a technical term (as its equivalent was in Plato's and Aristotle's), and that he very emphatically did not claim that Ideas—another technical term—"are identical with the things in flux."

The dictum around which these misinterpretations have been woven most persistently, beginning when Hegel was still alive, occurs in the Preface to his *Philosophy of Right* and reads: "What is rational, is actual; and what is actual, is rational."

This dictum is very simular to Leibniz's idea that this world is the best of all possible worlds. Without sympathizing in the least with either of these two ideas, one should realize that both are rooted in religion. In the third edition of his *Encyclopaedia* (1830; § 6) Hegel himself said of his epigram:

> These simple sentences have seemed striking to some and have excited hostility—even from people who would not wish to deny some understanding of philosophy, not to speak of religion. . . . When I have spoken of actuality, one might have inquired, without being told to do so, in what sense I use this expression; after all, I have treated actuality in an elaborate *Logic* and there distinguished it precisely not only from the accidental, which, of course, has existence, too, but also, in great detail, from being there, existence, and other concepts.

Alas, this passage was not included in *Scribner's Selections;* hence these distinctions are overlooked by Popper, who reiterates the popular myth that, according to Hegel, "everything that is now real or actual . . . must be reasonable as well as good. And particularly good is, as we shall see, the actually existing Prussian state."

It would prevent some confusion if Hegel's term *wirklich* were translated *actual*, seeing that he opposed it to *potential* rather than to *unreal* or *nonexistent*. An acorn, though certainly real enough in the usual sense of that word, is not, as Hegel uses that term, *wirklich*. Only that is actual in Hegel's sense which fully realizes its own nature or, as Hegel might say, the "idea" of which most existent things fall short. And the Prussian state, though, according to Hegel, more rational than a state that is based on slavery, yet fell short in some respects, as his *Philosophy of Right* makes clear, of the "idea" of the state.

8. THE STATE

When Hegel speaks of "the State" he does not mean every state encountered in experience. Immediately after first offering his epigram about the rational and actual, he himself continued:

> What matters is this: to recognize in the semblance of the temporal and transient the substance which is immanent and the eternal which is present in it. For the rational (which is synonymous with the Idea), in its actuality, also embeds itself in external existence and thus manifests itself in an infinite wealth of forms, appearances, and figures, shrouding its core in a multicolored rind. Our consciousness first dwells on this rind, and only after that does philosophic thinking penetrate it to detect the inward pulse and to perceive its beat even in the external forms. The infinitely varied relations, however, which take shape in this externality . . . this infinite material and its organization are not the subject matter of philosophy.

Thus Hegel would distinguish between the Idea of the State, which he means when he speaks of "the State," and the many states around us. But the Idea, he claims, does not reside in a

Platonic heaven, but is present, more or less distorted, in these states. The philosopher should neither immerse himself in the description and detailed analysis of various historical states, nor turn his back on history to behold some inner vision: he should disentangle the rational core from the web of history.

Hegel is not driven to "juridical positivism" and the approbation of every state with which he is confronted, as Popper supposes (p. 252): he can pass judgment. Hegel makes a sharp distinction between such philosophic judgment and the arbitrary criticisms that reflect personal idiosyncrasies and prejudicies. This would not involve any difficulty if he were willing to restrict himself to internal criticism, pointing out the multifarious inconsistencies that are so striking in the utterances of most statesmen, in the platforms of most parties, and in the basic convictions of most people. Hegel, however, goes further.

He believes in a rational world order and in his ability to understand it. For him, life is not "a tale told by an idiot"; and history, not merely, although also, a succession of tragedies. There is an ultimate purpose—freedom—and this furnishes a standard of judgment.

A few quotations from the *Philosophy of Right* may illustrate this. "One may be able to show how a law is completely founded in, and consistent with, both circumstances and existing legal institutions, and yet is truly illegitimate and irrational" (§ 3). Hegel also speaks of "*unalienable*" rights and condemns, without qualification,

> slavery, serfdom, the disqualification from holding property or the prevention of its use or the like, and the deprivation of intelligent rationality, of morality, ethics, and religion, which is encountered in superstition and the concession to others of the authority and full power to determine and prescribe for me what actions I am to perform . . . or what duties my conscience is to demand from me, or what is to be religious truth for me [§66]

According to the addition of Gans, the editor, Hegel remarked in his lectures in this connection that "the slave has an absolute right to liberate himself" (cf. also § 77).

Hegel is not inconsistent when he writes: "the State cannot recognize conscience [*Gewissen*] in its peculiar form, i.e., as subjective knowledge [*Wissen*], just as in science, too, subjective opinion, assurance, and the appeal to subjective opinion have no validity" (§ 137). Conscience is fallible; and, while no government or church has the right to dictate to our conscience, no government can afford to recognize conscience as a legal standard. As several of his interpreters have pointed out, Hegel, when he wrote the *Philosophy of Right,* was concerned about the recent assassination of the poet Kotzebue by a student who was convinced that the poet was a Russian spy and deserved death.

We are bound to misunderstand Hegel when we apply his remarks about conscience within the framework of the Nazi state. It would be more pertinent if we thought of the German Republic before 1933 and of the conscience of Hitler. For by "the State" Hegel means one in which freedom is realized and "a human being counts because he is a human being, not because he is a Jew, Catholic, Protestant, German, Italian, or the like"—and this "is of infinite importance" (§ 209; cf. § 270 n.). Hegel would consider rational the conscience of an opponent of Hitler who recognized his own absolute right to make himself free and to realize his unalienable rights—but not the conscience of a fanatic impelled by personal motives or perhaps by an equally objectionable ideology.

It is no wonder that the Nazis found small comfort in a book that is based on the conviction that "the hatred of law, of right made determinate by law, is the shibboleth which reveals, and permits us to recognize infallibly, fanaticism, feeblemindedness, and the hypocrisy of good intentions, however they may disguise themselves" (§ 258 n.). In his Preface, too, Hegel called the law "the best shibboleth to distinguish the false brothers and friends of the so-called people." One may agree with Herbert Marcuse when he says in *Reason and Revolution: Hegel and the Rise of Social Theory:* "There is no concept less compatible with Fascist ideology than that which founds the state on a universal and rational law that safeguards the interests of every individual, whatever the contingencies of his natural and social status" (pp. 180 f.).

In sum: Popper is mistaken when he says, like many another critic, that, according to Hegel, "the only possible standard of judgment upon the state is the world historical *success* of its actions" (p. 260). Success is not the standard invoked in the *Philosophy of Right* when Hegel speaks of "bad states." "The State" does not refer to one of "the things in flux," but to an Idea and a standard of judgment, to what states would be like if they lived up fully to their *raison d'être*. This reason is to be found partly "in a higher sphere" (§ 270) for which Hegel himself refers the reader to his system as outlined in his *Encyclopaedia*. The whole realm of Objective Spirit and human institutions that culminates in the State is but the foundation of a higher realm of Absolute Spirit that comprises art, religion, and philosophy.

The discussion of "the State" in the *Philosophy of Right* opens with the pronouncement: "The State is the actuality of the ethical idea." If he were a Platonist, he would mean justice; but Hegel means freedom: not that freedom from all restraints which, at its worst, culminates in anarchy, license, and bestiality, but, rather, man's freedom to develop his humanity and to cultivate art, religion, and philosophy. He considers the State supreme among human institutions because he would subordinate all such institutions to the highest spiritual pursuits and because he believes that these are possible only in "the State." He himself says: "To be sure, all great human beings have formed themselves in solitude—but only by assimilating what had already been created in the State."[1] One might nevertheless insist, as Hegel does not, that conformity should be discouraged beyond the necessary minimum, and one might dwell, as Nietzsche did half a century later, on the dangers of the State.

It would be absurd to represent Hegel as a radical individualist; but it is equally absurd to claim, as Popper does (p. 258), that Hegel's State is "totalitarian, that is to say, its might must permeate and control the whole life of the people in all its functions: 'The State is therefore the basis and center of all the concrete elements in the life of a people: of Art, Law, Morals, Religion, and Science.' " Popper's claim simply ignores Hegel's emphatic insistence on the sphere of "subjective freedom," which he himself considered a decisive advance over Plato. The quotation from Hegel, of course, does not at all prove the preceding contention: it means—and the context in the lectures on the *Philosophy of History* (Preface) makes this quite clear—that the State alone makes possible the development of art, law, morals, religion, and science. And Hegel's formulation here shows less the influence of Plato, whom Popper represents as a terrible totalitarian, than the impact of Pericles, whom Popper admires. The sentence Popper quotes could almost come from Thucydides' version of Pericles' most famous speech.

Hegel's philosophy is open to many objections, but to confound it with totalitarianism means to misunderstand it. Ernst Cassirer puts the matter very clearly in *The Myth of the State* (1946), a book dealing with much the same material as Popper's, but in a much more scholarly manner. His Hegel chapter ends: "Hegel could extol and glorify the state, he could even apotheosize it. There is, however, a clear and unmistakable difference between his idealization of the power of the state and that sort of idolization that is the characteristic of our modern totalitarian systems."

9. HISTORY

Hegel, like Augustine, Lessing, and Kant before him and Comte, Marx, Spengler, and Toynbee after him, believed that history has a pattern and made bold to reveal it. All these attempts are controversial in detail and questionable in principle; but a sound critique of Hegel should also take into account his remarkable restraint: he did not attempt to play the prophet and was content to comprehend the past.

Popper says that his own book could be "described as a collection of marginal notes on the development of certain historicist philosophies" (p. 4); and, as we have seen, he accuses Hegel of "hysterical historicism." But according to Popper's definition, Hegel was no historicist at all: he was not one of those who "believe that they have discovered laws of history which enable them to prophesy the course of historical events." This addiction to predictions is what Popper means by historicism (p. 5).

We are told that Hegel was guilty of

historical and evolutionary relativism—in the form of the dangerous doctrine that what is believed today is, in fact, true today, and in the equally dangerous corollary that what was true yesterday (*true* and not merely "believed") may be false tomorrow—a doctrine which, surely, is not likely to encourage an appreciation of the significance of tradition [p. 254].

Hegel, of course, excelled in his appreciation of the significance of tradition; in his books and lectures he took for granted its essential rationality, and he condemnded as arbitrary any criticism of the past or present that was not accompanied by an appreciation of the significance of tradition.

He did not maintain "that what is believed today is, in fact, true today" but insisted that many of his contemporaries, both philosophers and "men in the street," held many mistaken beliefs. And "what was true yesterday . . . may be false tomorrow" is, in a sense, a commonplace—as when we take such statements as "it is raining" or "the Americans, while saying that all men are endowed by their Creator with certain unalienable rights, including liberty, hold slaves" or "another war might well spread the ideals of the French Revolution, without endangering the future of civilization." The same consideration applies to many a generalization about a nation and about war.

Hegel did not believe that such propositions as "two plus two equals four" were true at one time but not at another; he thought that the truth comes to light gradually and tried to show this in his pioneering lectures on the history of philosophy. He emphasized not how utterly wrong his predecessors had been but how much truth they had seen; yet Plato's and Spinoza's truths were not "all of the truth" but were in need of subsequent qualification and amendment.

Hegel's approach is not amoral. Although he finds the aim of history in its "result" (p. 260) and considers the history of the world the world's court of justice (p. 233 and n. 11), he does not idolize success. His attitude depends on his religious faith that in the long run, somewhere, somehow freedom will and must triumph: *that* is Hegel's "historicism." Those of us who lack his confidence should still note that he does not believe that things are good because they succeed, but that they succeed because they are good. He finds God's revelation in history.

This point is best illustrated by Hegel's polemic against Von Haller in the *Philosophy of Right* (§ 258). Throughout, he tries to avoid the Scylla of that revolutionary lawlessness that he associates with Fries and the Wartburg festival and the Charybdis of conservative lawlessness that he finds in Von Haller's *Restauration der Staatswissenschaft*. He cites Von Haller (I, 342 ff.): "As in the inorganic world the greater represses the smaller, and the mighty, the weak, etc., thus among the animals, too, and then among human beings, the same law recurs in nobler forms." And Hegel interposes. "Perhaps frequently also in ignoble forms?" He then quotes Von Haller again: "This is thus the eternal, immutable order of God, that the mightier rules, must rule, and always will rule." And Hegel comments: "One sees from this alone, and also from what follows, in what sense might is spoken of here: not the might of the moral and ethical, but the accidental force of nature."

Popper quotes Hegel: "A people can only die a violent death when it has become naturally dead in itself" (p. 263); and Hegel continues, "as e.g. the German Imperial Cities, the German Imperial Constitution" (n. 77). Applied to the collapse of the Holy Roman Empire in 1806, Hegel's remark makes sense, while his bold generalization invites criticism. But one should take into account that Hegel is in agreement with a religious tradition that extends from Isaiah to Toynbee.

Intent on dissociating Hegel from this religious tradition and on associating him with the Nazis instead, Popper fastens on Hegel's conception of world-historical peoples. He quotes (p. 258) Hegel's *Encyclopaedia* (§ 550) as saying that "the Spirit of the Time invests its Will" in "the self-consciousness of a particular Nation" that "dominates the World." This would seem to be another instance where Popper improved a translation without checking the original (cf. section 5 above). The passage in the *Encyclopaedia* reads: "The self-consciousness of a particular people is the carrier of the current stage of development of the universal spirit as it is present, and the objective actuality into which this spirit lays its will." In *Scribner's Hegel Selections,* this becomes ". . . in which that spirit for a time invests its will." And in Popper, finally, we suddenly encounter "the Spirit of the Time." His profuse capitalization of nouns in his quotations from Hegel is apparently intended to make Hegel look silly.

Hegel goes on to say, though Popper does not quote this, that the spirit "steps onward" and "delivers it over to its chance and doom." His position depends on his assumption that ultimate reality is spiritual and that the spirit reveals itself progressively in history. The stages of this revelation are represented by different peoples, but by only one people at any one time.

This strange notion was adapted by Stefan George and, with the individual prophet in the place of a whole people, became part of the creed of his Circle:

> *In jeder ewe*
> *Ist nur ein gott und einer nur sein künder.*

This idea that "in every epoch, there is but one god, and but one his prophet" is even more obviously false than Hegel's view; and it is doubly ironical because, even in the relatively small field of German poetry, George was no solitary giant but was eclipsed by his contemporary, Rilke.

Hegel's notion was surely suggested to him by the way in which the Romans succeeded the Greeks—and perhaps also the Greeks, the Persians; and the Persians, the Babylonians.

> This people is the *dominant* one in world history for this epoch— *and it can be epoch-making in this sense only once.* Against this absolute right which it has to be the embodiment of the current stage of development of the world spirit, the spirits of the other peoples have no right, and they, even as those whose epoch has passed, do not any longer count in world history.[2]

Above all, Hegel was probably also influenced by the Christian conception of the relation of Christianity to Jew and Greek.

Hegel's conception is dated today: we know more than he did about the history of a great number of civilizations. We can no longer reduce world history to a straight line that leads from the Greeks via the Romans to ourselves; nor can we dispose of ancient Asia as "The Oriental Realm" and understand it simply as the background of the Greeks. We are also aware of ambiguities in the conception of a *Volk* or nation and should not apply such terms to the carriers of Greek or Roman civilization. We understand the flowering of medieval philosophy in terms of the interaction of Jews, Muslims, and Christians against a Greek background, and should not care to say who in that epoch represented the world spirit. Some of us have even lost all belief in a world spirit.

All this does not imply that Hegel's views are wicked or that his basic error is due to his alleged nationalism or tribalism. Toynbee's conception of separate civilizations is open to almost the same objections.

With the exception of entirely isolated communities, no unit can be understood completely without reference to others. But any unit whatever, whether it be Western civilization, France, Athens, or the Burlington Railroad, can be made the object of a historical study. In each instance, one will introduce other units as sparingly as possible and only to throw light on the history of the unit under consideration.

Hegel's whole conception of "world history" is arbitrary and amounts to an attempt to study the development of his own civilization. But here he was at one with almost all of his contemporaries and predecessors who were also under the influence of the Bible. For it is from the Bible that the Western idea that history has a single beginning and moves along a single track toward a single goal received its impetus and sanction. Today we are apt to be more agnostic about the beginning; we are bound to deny the single track; but we may once again think in another sense of the unity of world history— a unity that is established by the present confluence of hitherto independent streams.

Hegel was not impeded by the recognition that some of the ancestors of his own civilization had made their epoch-making contributions simultaneously. Homer may have been a contemporary of the earliest prophets; Thales and Jeremiah wrote at the same time; and Stoicism flourished while Christianity developed out of Judaism. Elsewhere, Confucius and the Buddha were contemporaries. A pluralistic perspective is needed, as is more respect for individual units. There is no single plan into which all data can be fitted, and Hegel was certainly something of a Procrustes.

Any attempt, however, to read into Hegel's conception of "world domination" an exclusively political or even military sense in order to link him with Hilter is quite illegitimate. It is doubly misleading when one does not emphasize that Hegel was not making predictions or offering suggestions for the future but was scrupulously limiting himself to an attempt to understand the past. Pedagogically, the single-track conception has the virtue of simplicity; and it is still adopted almost universally in the field of Hegel's primary competence—the history of philosophy.

10. GREAT MEN AND EQUALITY

Hegel's conception of world-historical peoples is closely related to his notion of world-historical personalities. Both notions are justifiable up to a point. Some peoples have had little effect on anybody outside themselves, while the Greeks and the Jews, for example, have affected the history of the world out of all proportion to their numbers. Similarly, Socrates and Caesar might well be called world-historical personalities.

It is the rankest emotionalism when Popper writes:

> Glory cannot be acquired by everybody; the religion of glory implies antiequalitarianism—it implies a religion of "Great Men." Modern racialism accordingly "knows no equality between souls, no equality between men" (Rosenberg). Thus there are no obstacles to adopting the Leader Principles from the Arsenal of the perennial revolt against freedom, or as Hegel calls it, the idea of the World Historical Personality [pp. 266 f.]

Popper implies that we ought to be "for" equalitarianism; but if it involves the belief that no man can achieve anything that cannot be achieved by everybody else, too, it is simply silly. In any sense in which it is at all worth while, equalitarianism is entirely compatible with belief in great men.

According to Popper,

> Hegel twists equality into inequality: "That the citizens are equal before the law," Hegel admits, "contains a great truth. But expressed in this way, it is only a tautology; it only states in general that a legal status exists, that the laws rule. But to be more concrete, the citizens . . . are equal before the law only in the points in which they are equal *outside the law* also. *Only that equality which they possess in property, age, . . . etc., can deserve equal treatment before the law.* . . . The laws themselves presuppose unequal conditions. . . . It should be said that it is just the great development and maturity of form in modern states which produces the supreme concrete inequality of individuals in actuality" [p. 239].

The omissions in the Hegel quotation are Popper's, and Popper explains them in the very next sentence:

> In this outline of Hegel's twist of the "great truth" of equalitarianism into its opposite, I have radically abbreviated his argument; and I must warn the reader that I shall have to do the same throughout the chapter; for only in this way is it at all possible to present, in a readable manner, his verbosity and the flight of his thoughts (which, I do not doubt, is pathological).

A look at the *Encyclopaedia* (§ 539) shows that Hegel is not "for" or "against" equality but tries to determine in what sense it can be embodied in the modern state.

> With the appearance of the State, inequality enters; namely, the difference between the governing forces and the governed, authorities, magistrates, directories, etc. The principle of equality, carried out consistently, would repudiate all differences and thus be at odds with any kind of state.

It is in the following discussion that we find the sentence italicized by Popper, and it seems best to quote it without omissions and with Hegel's, rather than Popper's, italics:

> Only that equality which, in whatever way, *happens to exist independently,* regarding wealth, age, physical strength, talents, aptitude, etc., or also crimes, etc., can and should justify an equal treatment of these before the law—in regard to taxes, liability to military service, admission to public office, etc., or punishment, etc.

Hegel's sentence, though hardly elegant, is carefully constructed and exhibits a crucial parallelism. Only those with equal wealth should be taxed equally; age and physical strength should be taken into account by draft boards; talents and aptitudes are relevant qualifications for public service; and so forth. Or should we have equal punishment for all, regardless of whether they have committed equal crimes? Should we induct children into the armed forces and exact equal taxes from the poor and the rich? Is it Hegel that is guilty of a "twist"?

To return to "great men": Hegel said, according to Gans's addition to section 318: "Public opinion contains everything false and everything true, and to find what is true in it is the gift of the great man. Whoever tells his age, and accomplishes, what his age wants and expresses, is the great man of his age." (Popper's "translation" of this passage [p. 267] makes nonsense of it: "In public opinion of all is false and true. . . .") Hegel's passage ends, in Popper's translation: "He who does not understand *how to despise public opinion,* as it makes itself heard here and there, will never accomplish anything great."

Popper's italics as well as his comments appeal to the reader's prejudice in favor of the supremacy of public opinion, though he previously appealed to the prejudice in favor of the supremacy of conscience. These two standards, however, are very different; and Hegel recognized the fallibility of both because he did not believe, as Popper alleges (p. 237), that "self-evidence is the same as truth." Hegel argued, in the body of section 318, that "to be independent of [public opinion] is the first formal condition of anything great and rational"; and he had the faith that public opinion "will eventually accept it, recognize it, and make it one of its own prejudices."

In the above quotation from Gans's addition, Popper finds an "excellent description of the Leader as a publicist"; and since he has introduced it with a reference to "the Leader principle," one is led to think of the *Führer* and to consider Hegel a proto-Nazi. The quotation, however, is not at odds with a sincere belief in democracy and fits beautifully not only Franklin D. Roosevelt's "interventionism" but also Lincoln's great speeches; for example, "A house divided against itself cannot stand" or "With malice toward none; with charity for all." And it is true of Lincoln, too, when Hegel says of the world-historical personalities, "They were practical, political men. But at the same time they were thinking men, who had an insight into the requirements of the time—into what was ripe for development."

Hegel found that world-historical individuals are always propelled by some passion ("Nothing Great in the World has been accomplished without *passion*") and that their motivation is rarely entirely disinterested. The latter point he expressed in terms of "the cunning of reason." The individual may be motivated not only by profound insights but also by "private interests" and even "self-seeking designs." Alexander was passionately ambitious; but in the long run his private interests furthered Western civilization. The same consideration applies to Caesar and to Franklin D. Roosevelt; in *The American Political Tradition,* Richard Hofstadter has shown how Lincoln, too, was fired by political ambitions until he was elected president.

Popper links Hegel with "the fascist appeal to 'human nature' [which] is to our passions" and proposes that we call this appeal the "*cunning of the revolt against reason*" (p. 268). Yet he himself evidently believes that Napoleon, whose motivation was hardly entirely disinterested and whose methods could scarcely be approved by a devotee of "the open society," was furthering Western civilization to such an extent that the German uprising against him must be labeled "one of these typical tribal reactions against the expansion of a supernational empire" (p. 250).

11. WAR

Without accepting Hegel's view of war, one should distinguish it clearly from the Fascists'. Three points may suffice here.

First, Hegel looks back, not forward. He is not less interested than Popper in "the furthering of civilization" (p. 268) but finds that our civilization has been furthered by any number of wars in the past; for example, the Greeks' war against the Persians, Alexander's wars of conquest, some of the Romans' wars, and Charlemagne's conquest of the Saxons. Believing that it is the philosopher's task to comprehend "that which is"—to cite the Preface to the *Philosophy of Right*—and not to construct utopias, Hegel speaks of war as one of the factors that have actually furthered civilization.

Second, we should not confuse Hegel's estimate of the wars that had occurred up to his own time with a celebration of war as we know it today or imagine it in the future.

Third, Hegel's attitude is not fully comprehensible when considered apart from its religious roots. He considered all that is finite ephemeral. According to Gans's addition to section 324, he said: "From the pulpits much is preached concerning the insecurity, vanity, and instability of temporal things, and yet everyone . . . thinks that he, at least, will manage to hold on to his possessions." What the preachers fail to get across, "Hussars with drawn sabres" really bring home to us. (Popper writes "glistening sabres" [p. 269]; and the change, though slight, affects the tone of the passage.)

These three points are sufficient to show how Popper misrepresents Hegel's view. "Hegel's theory," we are told, "implies that war is good in itself. 'There is an ethical element in war,' we read" (p. 262). This is a curious notion of implication: from Hegel's contention that "there is an ethical element in war, which should not be considered an absolute evil" (§ 324), Popper deduces that Hegel considered war "good in itself." Hegel attempted to solve the problem of evil by demonstrating that even evil serves a positive function. He accepted Goethe's conception of "that force which would/Do evil evermore and yet creates the good." It is of the very essence of Hegel's dialectical approach to penetrate beyond such assertions as that war is good or evil to a specification of the respects in which it is good and those in which it is evil. Today the evil so far outweighs any conceivable good that we are apt to be impatient with anyone who as much as mentions any good aspects; but in a concrete predicament, the majority still feels that the good outweighs the evil, even if this point is made by speaking of "the lesser evil."

The one passage in which Hegel does consider the question of future wars is not well known and is worth quoting. It is found in his Berlin lectures on aesthetics:

> Suppose that, after having considered the great epics of the past [the *Iliad, Cid,* and Tasso's, Ariosto's, and Camoëns' poems], which describe the triumph of the Occident over the Orient, of European measure, of individual beauty, and of self-critical reason over Asiatic splendor, . . . one now wished to think of great epics which might be written in the future: they would only have to represent the victory of the living rationality which may develop in America, over the incarceration into an infinitely progressing measuring and particularizing. For in Europe every people is now limited by another and may not, on its part, begin a war against another European people. If one now wants to go beyond Europe, it can only be to America.[3]

In his lectures on the philosophy of history, Hegel also hailed the United States as "the land of the future."[4] Plainly, he did not believe that world history would culminate in Prussia. His lectures on history do not lead up to a prediction but to the pronouncement: "To this point consciousness has come."

This may also be the clue to the famous expression of resignation at the end of the Preface to the *Philosophy of Right*—a passage that, at first glance, seems at odds with the subsequent demand for trial by jury and for a real parliament with public proceedings, institutions then still lacking in Prussia. But apparently Hegel did not believe that Prussia, or Europe, had any real future: "When philosophy paints its grey on grey, a form of life has grown old, and with grey on grey it cannot be rejuvenated, but only comprehended. The owl of Minerva begins its flight only at dusk."

12. NATIONALISM

On this point Popper's account is particularly confused. "When nationalism was revived a hundred years ago [about 1850?], it was in one of the most mixed regions of Europe, in Germany, and especially in Prussia" (p. 245). A page later, we hear of "the invasion of German lands by the first national army, the French army under Napoleon." Three pages later we are told that Fichte's "windbaggery" gave "rise to modern nationalism." Fichte died in 1814. Contemptuous of the concept of nationality, Popper maintains that it is a common belief in democracy, "which forms, one might say, the uniting factor of multilingual Switzerland" (p. 246). Why, then, have the Swiss no wish to unite with any democratic neighbor? Popper's opposition to many features of modern nationalism is well taken; but those who are interested in its development, or who wish to understand it, will do better to turn to Hans Kohn's *The Idea of Nationalism* (1944) and to his chapter on "Nationalism and the Open Society" in *The Twentieth Century* (1949).

One of the major themes of Popper's Hegel chapter is that "Hegelianism is the renaissance of tribalism" (p. 226). Popper's use of "tribalism" and "nationalism" is emotional rather than precise, and he accuses Hegel of both. Even so he must admit that Hegel "sometimes attacked the nationalists" (p. 251). Popper cites Hegel's *Encyclopaedia* where the so-called nation is condemned as rabble:

> And with regard to it, it is the one aim of a state that a nation should *not* come into existence, to power and action, as such an aggregate. Such a condition of a nation is a condition of lawlessness, demoralization, brutishness. In it, the nation would only be a shapeless wild blind force, like that of a stormy elemental sea, which however is not self-destructive, as the nation—a spiritual element—would be.

The Nazis concluded quite correctly that Hegel was unalterably opposed to their conception of the *Volk* and his idea of the State was its very antithesis.[5]

Popper, on the other hand, is so intent on opposing Hegel that he immediately seeks to enlist the reader's sympathies on the nationalist side when he finds Hegel criticizing it. Thus Popper is not content to point out, quite correctly, that Hegel is referring "to the liberal nationalists" but must add, "whom the king hated like the plague." Hegel's attitude, of course, cannot be understood or reasonably evaluated in terms of the emotional impact of such words as "liberal" and "king." What is wanted is a profile of the movement condemned by Hegel; and that may be found in Herbert Marcuse's *Reason and Revolution* (pp. 179 f.):

> There was much talk of freedom and equality, but it was a freedom that would be the vested privilege of the Teutonic race alone. . . . Hatred of the French went along with hatred of the Jews, Catholics, and "nobles." The movement cried for a truly "German war," so that Germany might unfold "the abundant wealth of her nationality." It demanded a "savior" to achieve German unity, one to whom "the people will forgive all sins." It burned books and yelled woe to the Jews. It believed itself above the law and the constitution because "there is no law to the just cause." The state was to be built from "below," through the sheer enthusiasm of the masses, and the "natural" unity of the *Volk*

was to supersede the stratified order of state and society. It is not difficult to recognize in these "democratic" slogans the ideology of the Fascist *Volksgemeinschaft*. There is, in point of fact, a much closer relation between the historical role of the *Burschenschaften,* with their racism and antirationalism, and National Socialism, than there is between Hegel's position and the latter. Hegel wrote his *Philosophy of Right* as a defense of the state against this pseudo-democratic ideology.

The "liberal" Fries called for the extermination of Jewry (section 5 above), while Hegel denounced the nationalistic clamor against the extention of civil rights to the Jews, pointing out that this "clamor has overlooked that they are, above all, human beings" (§ 270 n.). Are we to condemn Hegel because he agreed with the king, or praise Fries because he called himself liberal?

Popper's most ridiculous claim—and the last one to be considered here—is that the Nazis got their racism from Hegel. In fact, the Nazis did not get their racism from Hegel, and Hegel was no racist (see section 5 above).

The Nazis did find some support for their racism in Schopenhauer, with whom Popper constantly makes common cause against Hegel, and in Richard Wagner, who Popper eccentrically insinuates was something of a Hegelian (p. 228) though he was, of course, a devoted disciple of Schopenhauer. Popper declares that one W. Schallmeyer, when he wrote a prize essay in 1900, "thus became the grandfather of racial biology" (p. 256). What, then, is the status of the rather better known and more influential Gobineau and Chamberlain and any number of other writiers who publicized their views before 1900 and were widely read and constantly quoted by the Nazis?

Popper offers us the epigram: "Not 'Hegel + Plato,' but 'Hegel + Haeckel' is the formula of modern racialism" (p. 256). Why Haeckel rather than Bernhard Förster, Julius Langbehn, Hofprediger Stöcker, Chamberlain, Gobineau, or Wagner? Why not Plato, about whose reflections on breeding the Nazis' leading race authority, Dr. Hans F. K. Günther, wrote a whole book—and Günther's tracts on race sold hundreds of thousands of copies in Germany and went through several editions even before 1933? (See section 5 above.) And why Hegel?

Decidedly, Hegel was no racialist; nor does Popper adduce any evidence to prove that he was one. Instead, Popper says: "The transubstantiation of Hegelianism into racialism or of Spirit into Blood does not greatly alter the main tendency of Hegelianism" (p. 256). Perhaps the transubstantiation of God into the *Führer* does not greatly alter Christianity?

One can sympathize with G. R. G. Mure when he says that the increasingly violent and ill-informed attacks on Hegel have reached a point in Popper's Hegel chapter where they become "almost meaninglessly silly."[6] But familiarity with Hegel has waned to the point where reviewers of the original edition of *The Open Society and Its Enemies,* while expressing reservations about the treatment of Plato and Aristotle, have not generally seen fit to protest against the treatment of Hegel; and on the jacket of the English edition Bertrand Russell actually hails the attack on Hegel as "deadly"—for Hegel. Since the publication of the American edition in 1950, John Wild and R. B. Levinson have each published a book to defend Plato against the attacks of Popper and other like-minded critics, and Levinson's *In Defense of Plato* goes a long way toward showing up Popper's methods. But Popper's ten chapters on Plato, although unsound, contain many excellent observations, and his book is so full of interesting discussions that no exposé will relegate it to the limbo of forgotten books. *The Open Society* will be around for a good long while, and that is one reason why its treatment of Hegel deserves a chapter.

What is ultimately important is not the failing of one author but the increasing popularity of the Hegel myth and of the methods on which it depends. To cite Nietzsche's *Ecce Homo* once more: "I only avail myself of the person as a magnifying glass with which one can render visible a general but creeping calamity which it is otherwise hard to get hold of."

Popper should be allowed the last word. And any critic of his work could do worse than to cite in his own behalf what Popper says to justify his own critique of Toynbee:

> I consider this a most remarkable and interesting book. . . . He has much to say that is most stimulating and challenging. . . . I also agree with many of the political tendencies expressed in his work, and most emphatically with his attack upon modern nationalism and the tribalist and "archaist," i.e., culturally reactionary tendencies, which are connected with it. The reason why, in spite of this, I single out . . . [this] work in order to charge it with irrationality, is that only when we see the effects of this poison in a work of such merit do we fully appreciate its danger (pp. 435 f.).

NOTES

1. *Die Vernunft in der Geschichte,* ed. Lasson, p. 92; *Reason in History,* transl. Hartman, p. 51.
2. *Philosophy of Right,* § 347.
3. *Werke,* ed. Glockner, XIV, 354 f.
4. *Ibid.,* XI, 128 f.
5. Cf. e.g., Rosenberg's *Mythus,* (1940 ed.), p. 527.
6. *A Study of Hegel's Logic,* p. 360.

FOR FURTHER READING

Avineri, Shlomo. "The Problem of War in Hegel's Thought," in *Journal of the History of Ideas,* XXII: 4, 1961, 463–74.

———. "Hegel's Views on Jewish Emancipation," in *Jewish Social Studies,* XXV: 2, April 1963, 145–51.

Collingwood, R. G. *The Idea of History.* Oxford, 1946, pp. 113–26.

Findlay, J. N. *Hegel: A Re-examination,* 1958; Collier Books, 1962.

Foster, Michael B. *The Political Philosophies of Plato and Hegel.* Oxford, 1935.

Hegel, G. W. F. *Philosophy of Right.* tr. with notes by T. M. Knox. Oxford, Clarendon, 1942; Oxford paperback 1967.

———. *Political Writings.* tr. by T. M. Knox, with an Introductory Essay by Z. A. Pelczynski. Oxford, Clarendon, 1964.

Hook, Sidney. *From Hegel to Marx: Studies in the Intellectual Development of Karl Marx,* 1936; reprinted, New York, Humanities Press, 1950.

*Kaufmann, Walter. *Hegel: Reinterpretation, Texts, and Commentary,* Garden City, N.Y., Doubleday, 1965; Anchor Books paperback ed. in 2 vols., 1966.

———. *From Shakespeare to Existentialism,* 1959; "A New Edition, with Additions," Doubleday Anchor Books, 1960.

Marcuse, Herbert. *Reason and Revolution: Hegel and the Rise of Social Theory,* 1941, 2d ed., 1955; Beacon paperback, 1960.

* This volume contains a comprehensive bibliography (pp. 469–86) that includes Hegel's writings, both in German and in English, as well as writings about Hegel.

Index

ΦA